Created and Directed by Hans Höfer

INSIGHT GUIDES
PUERTO RICO

Edited by Chris Caldwell and Tad Ames
Principal photography by Bill Wassman
Updated by Larry Luxner

Editorial Director: Brian Bell

HOUGHTON MIFFLIN COMPANY

APA PUBLICATIONS

PUERTO RICO

Second Edition
© **1995 APA PUBLICATIONS (HK) LTD**
All Rights Reserved
Printed in Singapore by Höfer Press Pte Ltd

Distributed in the United States by:	Distributed in Canada by:	Distributed in the UK & Ireland by:	Worldwide distribution enquiries:
Houghton Mifflin Company	**Thomas Allen & Son**	**GeoCenter International UK Ltd**	**Höfer Communications Pte Ltd**
222 Berkeley Street	390 Steelcase Road East	The Viables Center, Harrow Way	38 Joo Koon Road
Boston, Massachusetts 02116-3764	Markham, Ontario L3R 1G2	Basingstoke, Hampshire RG22 4BJ	Singapore 2262
ISBN: 0-395-70063-9	ISBN: 0-395-70063-9	ISBN: 9-62421-045-4	ISBN: 9-62421-045-4

ABOUT THIS BOOK

The writer Nicholas Wollaston once described Puerto Rico as "a kind of lost love-child, born to the Spanish Empire and fostered by the United States." Those words were written over 30 years ago, but the sentiment still applies. The Puerto Rican Spanish mentality is ingrained with North American culture, and a love-hate relationship with Uncle Sam that is unresolved: a recent plebiscite came out against Puerto Rico becoming America's 51st state – but only just. Meanwhile, millions of Puerto Ricans work on the US mainland, and Puerto Rico's own economy continues to be supported by US tax breaks.

For the Puerto Rican nationalist the island-nation is in an impossibly frustrating situation; for the visiting traveler the island's cultural confusion is another attraction in a land that knows how to put together a cocktail, reckoning to have invented the *piña colada*. But Puerto Rico's richness and diversity does not lie only in its culture: the landscape, too, has a touch of everything, from dense mountainous tropical forests to azure Caribbean beaches, to arid flatlands and rugged *cordilleras*. And all within an island small enough to make it readily accessible to anyone with a sense of adventure – and a car; Puerto Rico is, after all, one of the world's top car ownership populations.

A Fresh Look

In its original form this book dates from Insight Guides' first forays into the Caribbean. Since then, Apa Publications has covered all the key Caribbean destinations in the Insight Guide series and has embarked on a new series of Insight Pocket Guides to further equip the visitor. Providing a choice of travel publications has become the concern of Apa Publications' innovative chairman, **Hans Höfer**, who himself created the first Insight Guide (Bali) in 1970, and who remains the driving force behind the company.

The new edition of this book was masterminded from Apa's London editorial office. US-born journalist **Larry Luxner**, long-term resident of San Juan, was commissioned to carry out the necessary revisions, to add new chapters and effectively renew the whole of the Travel Tips section. In addition to extensive updating and rewriting, Luxner wrote four new pieces for the book: on the drug business, the Arecibo Observatory, the Ponce Art Museum and the Tuna factories of Mayagüez. He and a regular Apa photographer, **Bill Wassman**, who did most of the original photography, provided replacements for any pictures that had become dated. A graduate of Indiana University, Wassman worked as an assistant to photographers Eric Meola and Pete Turner before establishing his own international reputation.

For the original *Insight Guide: Puerto Rico* Apa Publications called together the perfect team of experts and insiders. Harvard graduate **Christopher Caldwell** headed the project. Caldwell worked as a freelance journalist in England and the United States and had edited various guidebooks. He spent a considerable time in Puerto Rico, gathering material and contacting local writers and photographers, as well as writing the chapters on San Juan, the Northwest and the Southeast, and destinations on the Northeast.

Project co-editor **Tad Ames** pulled the raw material of the book into its final form, seeing to the details needed to ready the book for

Sarah & Chris Caldwell

Luxner

Wassman

Cherson

publication. After graduating from Yale University, he spent a year reporting police news for a small daily newspaper in Connecticut. He then went to work as an editorial writer for the Berkshire *Eagle* based in Pittsfield, Massachusets.

Sarah Ellison Caldwell, whose marriage to Christopher Caldwell temporarily interrupted the book's production, spent long hours in Cambridge libraries shaping her history of Puerto Rico. She also wrote the article on rum. A Harvard graduate, she is the author of *Instruments of Conquest*, a comparison of British and Spanish colonial policies in the American Southeast.

Webster and **Robert Stone** are San Franciscans who covered the Northeast and Islands. **Angelo Lopez**, a Texan and like Webster a Harvard graduate, spent a number of weeks crossing Puerto Rico in a rented Mitsubishi, capturing the rugged contours of the Cordillera Central in his well-honed prose. A published writer of fiction, Lopez lives in Los Angeles, where he writes screenplays.

San Juan native **Adam Cherson** is an actor and writer living in New York. After graduating from Harvard, Cherson worked as a consultant in arts management and wrote the feature on language. He also delved into his leviathan salsa collection to research "Salsa: Rhythm of the Tropics."

Kathleen O'Connell, co-author with Luxner of the feature on People and Society in Puerto Rico, is, in the Puerto Rican lexicon, a part-time Continental. O'Connell is the arts editor of the Middletown (Connecticut) *Press*, but she spends every possible week on the island. Kathy has roots of her own on Puerto Rico: she graduated in 1966 from Academia San Ignacio.

Hanne-Maria Maijala attributes her taste for the balmier climes to having grown up in Finland and Canada. She graduated from Harvard after editing a literary journal, playing rugby, and completing her B.A. in French and English literature. Since then, she has done editorial work for Little, Brown & Co. in Boston, and went on to work as a financial analyst in New York.

Eleanora Abreau Jimenez, who wrote the feature on Puerto Rican cuisine, is a native of Guaynabo, Puerto Rico, studying medicine at the University of Puerto Rico at Río Piedras. Abreau attended Tulane University. **Susan Hambleton** ("Island Art"), is an artist from New York who has traveled extensively in Puerto Rico.

Behind the Scenes

Finally, without the assistance of **Adam Liptak**, the original book might have literally collapsed under its own weight. Liptak served as liaison between the various editors, authors and publisher Höfer, while juggling academic responsibility at Yale Law School.

Other contributors and people who deserve special appreciation, having helped in one way or another for the original edition, are, Richard Lamb, Ivan Damyanoff of Arrow Air; Thrifty Rent-a-Car, Irving Greenblatt of Casa del Frances, Jack Becker, Lorenzo Homar, Myrna Baez, Piana Espinosa, John F. Root, Jack Delano, Davey Jones, Sally, Allen and Taddeo of El Batey, Drew J. Guff, Eben W. Keyes, David and Phyllis Caldwell, and LeRoy and Kate Ellison.

This edition was co-ordinated by Insight Guides' London-based executive editor **Andrew Eames**, and was proof-read and indexed by **Mary Morton**.

W. Stone

R. Stone

O'Connell

Maijala

Hambleton

Introduction

History

Features

Places

Maps

TRAVEL TIPS

**For detailed information
see page 257**

A HEADY MIX

The island of Puerto Rico is 100 miles long and just 32 miles from north to south; if it were to be flattened, however, it would cover three times the area thanks to large areas of densely-forested mountains. This topography concentrates the population of 3.8 million in a few, very dense urban centers, where car ownership is sixth highest in the world. Meanwhile, up in the mountains, farming techniques haven't changed for 500 years.

Thanks to its varied landscape, the island has three different kinds of weather: a tropical climate on the beaches of the north coast, endless rains in the lush forests of the mountainous center, and a dry, arid heat along the southern coast. In fact, some people say that weather is born in Puerto Rico.

Puerto Rico overflows with traces of her past, in primitive carvings, in architecture, in cuisine and even in farming techniques. Here, everyone comes from somewhere else: the native population had all but vanished within a few years of Spanish colonisation, but centuries later, after the struggles of independence and power struggles with the Dutch and the English, Puerto Rico has arrived at a strange but fruitful relationship with the United States, with citizen status but no voting rights. This relationship is vital for Puerto Rico's economy, and 2½ million Puerto Ricans spend their working life on the mainland. But the island likes to keep its distance: in a recent referendum Puerto Rico decided against becoming America's 51st state.

Although Puerto Rico is predominantly Roman Catholic, spiritualism still flourishes. Saints are relied upon to keep the hurricanes away – not always successfully. The family unit is still key to local life, with Sunday picnics on the beaches a traditional pastime.

It's an enigmatic, spiritual, magical destination, where the familiar mixes completely naturally with the exotic. This distinctive, heady mix is examined, and celebrated, in the following pages.

Preceding pages: Veigante fiesta mask dancer; Playa Mar Chiquita, near Arecibo; San Cristóbal Canyon; San Cristóbal Castle, San Juan; surfing at Punta Higuero, Rincón. <u>Left</u>, welcome to Puerto Rico.

Within a year of his triumphant return to Spain with news of his discoveries, Christopher Columbus set sail across the Atlantic on a second voyage to the New World. This time, he traveled under orders of King Ferdinand and Queen Isabella to explore the hemisphere and claim the territories for the Spanish Crown. The "Catholic Monarchs" Ferdinand and Isabella had already secured the sole rights to the Americas – at least in the eyes of the Roman Catholic Church – by a series of Papal Bulls issued in 1493 which granted Spain "all islands and mainlands, discovered or yet to be discovered, sighted or not yet sighted" in the Western Hemisphere. Not only did Spain claim dominion over all the lands in the New World; the monarchs also had complete sovereignty over the Indians who lived there.

When Columbus discovered Puerto Rico on his second voyage in 1493, he found plenty of Taíno (also called Arawak) Indians already occupying the island. It has not yet been conclusively determined how or when the Taínos arrived, but much has been learned by the discovery at Loíza of a limestone cave containing artifacts of the early people. Carbon-dating reveals that the island has been occupied since the 1st century AD, and shells fashioned into gouging tools for use in the manufacture of dug-out canoes suggest that the first Indian rowed over from Venezuela, where similar relics have been recovered. There was unquestionably steady communication and trade between the islands. In his journal Columbus describes a Taíno canoe which seated three men abreast and 70 to 80 in all. "A barge could not keep up with them in rowing," he wrote, "because they go with incredible speed, and with these canoes they navigate among these islands."

Part of a well-defined Indian culture that originated in Hispaniola and extended throughout the Antilles, the Taíno in Puerto Rico lived in a rigidly stratified society. A great king lived on the island of Hispaniola and district caciques – chiefs – governed the

districts of Puerto Rico, which the Indians called *Borínquen* – "Island of the Brave Lord." Each district had a centrally located capital village where the *cacique* resided. As in medieval Europe, heredity determined status within society, which comprised *nitaínos*, or nobles who advised the *caciques* and enjoyed certain privileges; commoners; and *naborías,* or slaves.

Taíno villages ranged in size from a couple of hundred to a couple of thousand people. The Indians spent most of their time out-

of-doors, yet they did build large, campanulate thatch houses in which as many as 40 family members slept. The houses were built around a large open space reserved for public ceremonies and for *batey,* which the Spanish referred to as *pelota* – a ball game. The house of the *cacique* was the largest in town and always fronted on this public square. At Tibes, in Ponce, an Indian village has been reconstructed from ancient ruins.

The Taínos believed in a polytheistic order of creation. *Yocahú* was the Supreme Creator who commanded all the gods, the earth and all the creatures on it. The angry god of the winds, *Juracán*, invoked the eponymous hurricanes which disrupted island life from time to time. In the central square, the Indians observed religious worship and participated in ceremonial dances. Ceramic icons and clay idols in anthropological museums are evidence of the religious past. South of Arecibo, at the 13-acre Caguana Indian Ceremonial Park, used for religious purposes eight centuries ago, there are stone monoliths, 10 *bateyes* balls and other artifacts.

Traces of Taíno agriculture remain in Puerto Rico. Their ingenious method of sowing a variety of plants in earthen mounds called *conducos* is still employed by some farmers. The *conduco* system mitigated the problems of water distribution: water intensive crops were placed at the bottom and those requiring good drainage at the top. Cassava bread, the staple of the Taíno diet, was made by grating and draining the root which the Indians formed into loaves and baked. They also relied heavily upon yams – sweet *batates* and unsweet *ages* – and among the plant samples the early settlers sent back to Spain were maize, beans, squash and peanuts. Using *macanas*, stout double broadswords still used by Puerto Rican farmers, and pointed sticks, the Taínos cleared the thick woods and sowed their fields. Various sources of animal protein supplemented the starchy diet: fish from the Caribbean waters and sometimes pigeon or parrot.

In the time left over from farming, fishing and bagging small game, the Taínos developed various handicrafts. Early Spanish settlers in the region greatly admired the Indian woodwork: dishes, basins, bowls and boxes. Most prized of all were the ornate *duhos,* carved wooden thrones used by the *caciques.* The Great Taíno Cacique made a gift of a dozen of these to the Spanish Crown in the 1490s. Indian weavers used cotton and other fibrous plants to make colorfully dyed clothing, belts and hammocks. But the handicraft that aroused greatest excitement among the Spanish was the gold jewelry which the Indians wore as rings in their ears and noses. They neither mined nor panned for gold. When the Spaniards, smitten with desire for the precious metal, coaxed the natives into leading them to their sources, they were taken to beaches where gold nuggets from the ocean floor occasionally washed ashore.

Right, Taíno rock carvings, near Cayey.

JUAN PONCE DE LEON, SPANISH KNIGHT, DISCOVERER OF FLORIDA,
MARCH 27, 1513. AUTHENTIC PORTRAIT LOANED BY THE
ST. AUGUSTINE INSTITUTE OF SCIENCE AND HISTORICAL SOCIETY.

Fifteen years passed between the time of Columbus's discovery of the island of Borínquen on November 19, 1493, and serious attempts to settle it. The adventurer to the New World came across the island by chance during his second voyage while he was trying to reach Hispaniola. Renaming it San Juan Bautista, Columbus claimed it for the Spanish crown and promptly departed. From 1493 until 1508, the approximately 30,000 Taínos living on the island enjoyed a period of beneficient neglect: from time to time, Spaniards sailed to San Juan from Hispaniola seeking to barter for food. These encounters were always very friendly.

Enticing gold: One of the Spaniards who visited the island was Juan Ponce de León. The natives' ornaments and trinkets of gold caught Ponce's eye. He felt sure that the area was rich in gold and he secretly scouted the southern coast for sites for mines. In the early summer of 1508 Ponce de León and the Spanish governor of the Caribbean, Nicolas de Ovando, signed a clandestine agreement which granted Ponce de León rights to mine the island on the condition that he would yield two-thirds to the king. Secrecy was of utmost importance: Christopher Columbus's son, Diego Colón, had inherited the rights to exploit the island, but his family's monomaniacal desire for wealth had proved dangerous in the past. Physical abuse, dissolution of tribes and families and starvation of the Indians on Hispaniola had been followed by rebellion and bloodshed. Ponce de León and Ovando kept the deal quiet, hoping to avoid repetition of such a violent gold rush. Moreover, they were both well aware that the fewer who knew about the island's wealth, the larger the potential take for those who actually-- did.

In July 1508, Ponce de León and a band of 50 men – among them Luís de Añasco, the namesake of the river and village – set off for the island of San Juan Bautista. As they sailed eastward along the northern coast, they made friendly contact with the Indians, and Agueybaná, the head *cacique* of the

island, provided Ponce de León with an entry which ensured safe passage for him and his crew. Finally, after six weeks of searching, the explorers sighted a suitable site for settlement. In a valley several miles inland on an arm of the Bayamon River, Ponce de León founded the island's first European town, *Caparra* (a word that might be translated as "blossoming"). In official documents, it was referred to as *Ciudad de Puerto Rico*.

Relations between the Indians and the Europeans proceeded swimmingly. Panning

the river beds produced enough gold to persuade Ponce de León that the island merited permanent settlement. He had hoped for a small, strictly controlled group of Spaniards to live and work among the Indians without committing abuses or arousing hostility. However, as soon as King Ferdinand caught wind of Puerto Rico's excellent prospects, he directed a number of family friends there. Meanwhile, Diego Colón also entered the scene. Incensed that Ponce de León had grabbed the island for himself, he granted titles to two of his father's supporters – Cristóbal Sotomayor and Miguel Díaz – and subsidized their establishment on the island.

<u>Left</u>: **Ponce de León, the first Spanish governor.**
<u>Right</u>, **manuscript in San Juan's Casa del Libro.**

San Juan Bautista was now destined to suffer what Ponce de León had tried to avoid. By a colonial ordinance called a *repartimiento*, one of Colón's men enslaved 5,500 Indians ostensibly in order to convert them to Christianity but in reality to press them into labor.

The enslaved natives were divided and placed "under the protection" of 48 *hidalgos* (minor aristocracy, from *hijo de algo*, meaning "son of a somebody"). A combination of feudalism and capitalism, this was the *encomienda* system and it was employed throughout Spain's 16h-century New World empire. Across the northern coast the Spanish opened mines and panning operations, all supported by the free labor of the natives.

days of the initial outburst he and his captains had captured nearly 200 Indians, whom they subsequently sold into slavery, branding them on the face with the king's first initial. By June, peace once again reigned.

Unfortunately, the king felt sufficiently threatened by the rancorous Diego Colón that he had to acknowledge his claims. As a result, Ponce de León lost even more power. Colón's governmental appointments were recognized, and they continued to exploit the Indians according to the *encomienda* system. For a few years, the search for Puerto Rican gold continued at the expense of the Indians' freedom and until 1540, when the sources dried up, San Juan Bautista remained

The king appointed Ponce de León governor in 1510 but did not empower him to relinquish the *repartimiento*. The mining business proliferated, though there was so much competition for gold that the few who profited were men like Ponce de León who made their fortunes selling food and supplies to the miners. Moreover, not even Ponce de León could check the Spanish settlers' abuse of the Indians, especially in the remote western end of the island.

Indigenous resistance: During the winter of 1511, violence erupted and guerrilla warfare soon spread through the island. Ponce de León responded immediately. Within a few

one of the New World's foremost suppliers of gold to Spain. To assuage the wounded sensibilities of Juan Ponce de León for stripping his office down to little more than a title, King Ferdinand gave him permission to explore the virgin peninsula northwest of the Antilles which the Spanish called *La Florida*.

As people continued to immigrate to the island of San Juan Bautista they brought new commercial enterprises. The days when *hidalgos* left their homeland to strike it rich in New World gold mines were gone. Gradually, the settlers turned to agriculture as the mainstay of their economy. Land was plentiful and easy to come by, water was abundant and the climate mild. Labor posed a problem at first, for the Indians had disappeared quickly after the institution of the *repartimiento*. Epidemics of European diseases had swept through the communities of enslaved Indians, devastating the population. Those Indians who escaped fled into the mountainous interior or across the sea to join the tribes of coastal South America. However, West African blacks, imported by Portuguese slavers and supplied by the Spanish crown, provided an affordable replacement.

Peasant roots: Two sorts of farms developed. Some islanders, denied political and social status because they were *mestizos* (the progeny of a white and an Indian or black),

(born on the island) were chiefly interested in profit. After experimenting with a variety of crops, including ginger and tobacco, they finally settled on sugar as the most dependable and profitable cash crop. Sugar was relatively new to Europeans but their sweet tooth appeared to be insatiable. In 1516 entrepreneurs constructed the island's first *ingenio* – a factory in which raw cane is ground, boiled and reduced to sugar crystals. A decade and a half later, Puerto Rico sent its first sugar exports to Spain. King Charles V was so encouraged by it that he provided a number of technicians and loans for the industry's growth. Peripheral industries burgeoned as well: demand for timber to fuel the

were unable to obtain large land grants and credit. They resorted to subsistence farming and on their tiny plots raised cassava, corn, vegetables, fruit, rice and a few cattle. In general, *mestizos* cleared fields in inland regions that would not compete with the large coastal plantations. Puerto Rico's large peasant class blossomed from the seeds of these 16th-century subsistence farmers.

In addition there were, of course, owners of large plantations. Usually of purely European ancestry, these immigrants and Creoles

Left, the arrival of Christopher Columbus. **Above**, slave-labor created the plantations.

ingenios and food to fuel the laborers soared. Where sugar is processed, so inevitably is rum produced. Determined to squeeze all the profit possible out of their sugarcane, the Spanish settlers built distilleries soon after harvesting the first sugar crop.

By 1550, there were 10 active *ingenios* on the island, but the restrictive policies of the mercantilist king led to a crash in the market during the 1580s. Eventually the market recovered, but throughout Puerto Rico's history sugar would be not only one of the island's pre-eminent products, but also one of its most troubled industries.

Horses and husbandry: After the collapse of

the sugar trade, ginger emerged as the most successful product, and despite edicts from the monarch who preferred the cultivation of sugar, it flourished until the market bottomed out through a surplus. Animal husbandry was another lucrative industry. The armies that conquered Peru, Central America and Florida rode Puerto Rican horses. Island *hatos* (cattle ranches) supplied the local garrisons with meat for the troops.

The possibility of foreign aggression remained a constant threat. By the 1520s, the economic and strategic promise of the island – now officially called *Puerto Rico* – became apparent. Moreover, the individual with the clearest sense of Puerto Rico's potential and

Caca Fogo.   Caca Plata.

importance was gone. Juan Ponce de León had been fatally wounded in an encounter with Florida Indians in 1521; his remains are interred in the Metropolitan Cathedral of San Juan. Without a leader close to the Spanish king, defensive measures were hard to win.

In the year of Ponce de León's burial, the colonialists transferred the capital city from the site chosen by Ponce de León to a large natural bay to the north, renaming it San Juan. In the old riverbank town, mosquitoes had plagued settlers incessantly and the site proved too small to support increased river traffic as agriculture and industry developed. Advantageous as the new location was for

shipping, it left the people vulnerable to foreign invaders. In the 16th and 17th centuries, the French, English and Dutch dedicated themselves to unseating the powerful Habsburg monarchs both at home and abroad. As part of this campaign, they launched attack after attack on Spanish salients in the New World. Many of these attacks were carried out by privateers.

Fortifications: Encouraged by rumors of impending assault by French war vessels, San Juan officials in 1522 initiated construction of the port's first garrison. The wooden structure had not yet been completed before they realized it would be insufficient in the face of an attack. The island's first real defensive edifice was not completed until 1530, when descendants of Ponce de León built a house of stone, the Casa Blanca, designed to provide refuge for colonialists in the face of foreign aggression. The house still stands in Old San Juan. But not even the Casa Blanca fulfilled the defensive needs of the settlement, particularly given the expected large-scale population growth. Two years later, the army began building La Fortaleza, sometimes known as Santa Catalina. Today it houses the offices of the governor of Puerto Rico and it holds the distinction of being the oldest executive mansion in the Western Hemisphere.

The Fortaleza did little to supplement the defenses already provided by the Casa Blanca. Before it had been completed, army officers informed the crown that it had been built in "a poor place" and begged the appropriation of funds for another fortress. El Castillo de San Felipe del Morro (or, simply, *El Morro*) was the product of their entreaties. Placed on the rocky tip of the San Juan Peninsula, the fortification, which was finished in the 1540s, did much to assuage the fears of the northern capital's residents.

Meanwhile, the southwestern coastal settlement of San Germán fell victim to a series of raids by French corsairs over the next 30 years. Though their resistance could be compared to that of Texans at the Alamo, Spanish settlers were eventually overcome. San Germán was relocated 12 miles inland at its present site in Las Lomas, the hill country.

The French were not the only ones to attack Puerto Rican cities. The celebrated "sea dogs" of Queen Elizabeth, Sir Francis Drake and Captain John Hawkins, forcibly seized dozens of Spanish cargo ships traveling between the Antilles and Spain. In 1585, open war broke out between the two nations. England's well-known defeat of the Spanish *Armada Invincible* in 1588 left Spain permanently disabled as a naval power.

More defences: Towards the end of the 16th century, Puerto Rico received cursory attention. The Council of the Indies, the bureaucracy that oversaw the enforcement and administration of Spanish colonial policy in the Western Hemisphere, conferred upon the governor the title of Captain-General and directed him to improve the island's military preparedness. Governor Diego Menéndez de Valdes exercised tremendous initiative

was thwarted thanks to sturdy defenses. A historic confrontation in the autumn of 1594 resulted in an English defeat. During one of these battles, a cannon ball shot through the side of Francis Drake's ship and mortally wounded John Hawkins who was with Drake in his cabin. Drake was forced to retreat.

Yet the English would not give up. While the Spanish king nearly doubled to 409 the number of troops at the San Juan garrison of El Morro, the veteran sea warrior, George Clifford, third Earl of Cumberland, secretly planned an assault. He was aided by an influenza epidemic in 1598 which wiped out most of the able-bodied population of San Juan. As a result, the city was seriously

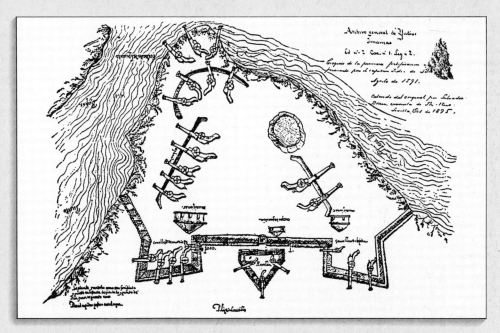

during the 1580s. A number of fortresses were constructed during his tenure including El Boquerón and Santa Elena in San Juan. Menéndez ordered the refurbishing of the land bridge La Puente de San Antonio – now La Puente de San Geronimo – and the strengthening of La Fortaleza. He also requisitioned artillery and ammunition, expanding the troop count from 50 to 209 men.

Menéndez stepped in just in the nick of time. A string of English assaults launched with the intention of capturing Puerto Rico

Left, foreign navies were a constant threat. Thus the heavy fortifications at El Morro (**Above**).

unprepared for the imminent attack.

Influenza's revenge: From a point 80 miles east of the capital, Cumberland's troops marched toward San Juan in June, easily taking fortifications as they proceeded. On July 1, the defenders who had been forced to hole up in El Morro surrendered the town. But the same scourge which had weakened the Puerto Ricans now struck the English conquerors. More than 400 English soldiers died of influenza within six weeks. The Puerto Ricans availed themselves of the British state of weakness. Refusing to acknowledge Cumberland's authority they engaged relentlessly in skirmishes on the outskirts of town. On August 27, Cumberland withdrew from the island, destroying two plantations in his wake.

Here the Dutch entered the picture. Determined to bring Spanish dominance of the Caribbean to an end, they commissioned Boudewijn Hendrikszoon to take over the island. Hendrikszoon's fleet of eight vessels arrived in San Juan harbor on September 24, 1625. In the course of the next three days, the Dutch slowly advanced, forcing a Spanish retreat into El Morro. The siege of San Juan lasted a month. Finally, the courageous Captains Juan de Amezquita and Andres Botello led surprise attacks on the Dutch trenches on October 22. The next 10 days of battle left the

Dutch fleet severely damaged – one ship destroyed and the troops depleted. The island was confirmed as a Spanish domain.

In the 1630s and 1640s, King Philip IV of Spain realized his plan to fortify the entire city of San Juan: seven fortresses were linked by a line of stone walls. The natives were inducted into the provincial district militia.

In control: Having seen off the English and the Dutch, the island was now relatively safe from invaders, and attentions were turned to the problem of establishing a strong economic base. But as a Spanish colony, Puerto Rico was allowed to keep open only one port – San Juan – and was barred from trading with non-Spanish powers. These strictures seriously limited the chances for economic growth. In the mid-16th century, when the influx of African slaves diminished, Britain threatened Spain on the high seas, and when non-Spanish producers in the West Indies developed more efficient sugar production, the sugar industry collapsed. Virtually nothing was exported in the 1560s and 1570s. In 1572 there was not a single ship in the harbor, and there was a seven-year span in which no European vessels docked at San Juan at all.

The Spanish crown, wishing to convert Puerto Rico into a defensive salient, instituted an assistance program called the *situado*. According to this plan, Puerto Rico was to receive from Mexico 2½ million *maravedies* annually. This was a substantial sum which should have been sufficient for the colonial government. However, the *situado* was a miserable failure. Privateers repeatedly intercepted it in transit and there was no way of ensuring it had been sent. While the delivery of bullion from Mexico was erratic, it did keep the island limping along until independent economic development began.

Smugglers all: Ironically, what turned the flagging island economy around was the circumvention of the Spanish mercantilist policies that were the cause of Puerto Rico's problems to begin with. Refused permanent concessions by the crown, the planters and merchants on Puerto Rico engaged increasingly in illicit foreign trade. Local produce – sugar, livestock, tobacco – was exchanged for slaves, staples, tools and other manufactured goods. By the mid-17th century almost everyone, from clerical authorities to soldiers, from friars to peasants, was involved in smuggling. The coastal towns of Aguada, Arecibo, Cabo Rojo and Fajardo grew into busy centers of illicit international trade.

Word of the proliferation of contraband activity and privateering in Puerto Rico eventually got back to Spain. Recognizing that the island's problems were critical, the king sent a commissioner, Alejandro O'Reilly, to evaluate the state of Puerto Rico. O'Reilly's report of 1765 was remarkably comprehensive and perspicacious. He reckoned the island's population had reached about 45,000: 40,000 freemen and 5,000 slaves. Most of the urban inhabitants lived in northeastern coastal towns and earned their livelihood through smuggling and blackmarket trade.

Smuggling was so prevalent that O'Reilly could report extensively on prices, supply, demand and distribution.

In 1765, a Spanish council met to review O'Reilly's report and to formulate a solution to the Puerto Rican problem. Recognizing the need for a stronger enforcement agent to curb contraband trade, they more than doubled the *situado* and installed as governor Don Miguel de Muesas. He was instructed to create a sturdy domestic economy. By building bridges and roads, by strengthening defenses, and by improving public education he hoped to promote agricultural prosperity and domestic self-sufficiency.

Despite the acuity with which O'Reilly pleaded Puerto Rico's case, Spain continued to see the development of the island's economy as secondary to its importance as the first naval fortification in her New World empire. Further, a population boom – largely attributable to immigration – had more than tripled the number of residents on the island by the turn of the century.

Meanwhile, Great Britain had her eye on Puerto Rico and was showing a readiness to acquire it. In 1797, after Napoleonic France and Spain had declared war on Britain, a British fleet of 60 vessels manned by 9,000 troops under the command of General Abercromby landed at Boca de Cangrejos. On April 17, they took Santurce and quickly laid siege upon the walled capital. Militia detachments from around the island arrived and launched a counter attack. Abercromby ordered a retreat on May 1.

Shifting control: Napoleon's invasion of Spain in 1808 sent shock waves through the empire and led to a complete reorganization of colonial rule. As control over the trans-Atlantic territories became weakened, several countries in the Americas won independence from Spain. A provisional assembly called the *Cortes* was convened in Spain to rule in the name of the deposed King Ferdinand VII. Fearing that Puerto Rican separatists who sympathized with the rebellious colonialists in South and Central America – Mexico and Venezuela particularly – would instigate revolutions at home, the *Cortes* invited Puerto Rico to send a delegation to Cádiz in 1809. An island Cre-

ole by the name of Ramón Power Giralt went as the colony's emissary and was elected vice president of the assembly. He pushed for reforms designed to ameliorate the social and economic ills of the island. Puerto Ricans gained status as Spanish citizens, tariffs on machinery and tools were dropped, a university was founded, and measures were taken to improve island industry. The *Cortes* disbanded in 1814 when Napoleon retreated and King Ferdinand VII returned to the throne. But the king, wary of the independence fever pervading the colonies, left in place a large fraction of Power's reforms in a *cédula de gracias* (royal decree) granted in 1815.

During the 10 years from 1795, trade be-

tween the United States and the Spanish West Indies grew by a factor of six. Household goods, food and, to a minor extent, slaves were supplied by the United States in exchange for West Indian staples such as sugar, coffee, rum and spices. In 1803 Puerto Rico sent 263,000 pounds of sugar to the United States and the amount exported grew yearly. In 1807 the US president, Thomas Jefferson, placed an embargo on all trade with the Spanish West Indies which cut exports by more than half. But after Napoleon Bonaparte's invasion of the Iberian peninsula, Jefferson lifted the embargo.

Not long after it was lifted, new difficul-

Left, Casa Blanca was Puerto Rico's first fort. Right, the patron saint of sailors.

ties floated into Puerto Rican harbors. Trying to respond to the threat Napoleon's armies posed on her borders, Spain called upon her colonies to ship an extraordinary supply of resources which could be used to outfit and maintain her own troops. With most profitable products going to Spain, Puerto Rico's economy suffered. And added to all these woes was the War of 1812 between Great Britain and the United States. The British blockade of the North American coast severely hampered American trade. Puerto Rico, by then one of the major suppliers of sugar to America, had nowhere to turn.

Increasing independence: The recovery following this tumultuous period included tremendous growth in the island economy. Ramón Power's economic reforms remained in place and for the first time since their institution began to have a real effect. Trade with the wealthy United States was not only permitted; the tariffs were decreased significantly. The *cédula de gracias* declared by Ferdinand VII in 1815 ended the Spanish trade monopoly in Puerto Rico by permitting trade with other countries. However, according to the dictates of the king, only Spanish vessels were allowed to carry on the exports. Once again, the colonial governors took exception to Spanish policy. Disobeying the king's orders, they gave right of entry to ships regardless of their origins. Also, under a civil intendancy plan instituted by Power, an independent official was appointed to oversee financial affairs, rather than leaving them in the hands of the governor. Alejandro Ramírez Blanco filled the post first. During his tenure he opened several ports, abolished superfluous taxes, and increased the export of cattle.

Between 1813 and 1818 Puerto Rican trade grew to eight times its previous level and in 1824 the king finally relinquished the last vestiges of mercantilism, conceding the right of Puerto Rican ports to harbor non-Spanish merchant ships. The future of the Puerto Rican economy became clear to many. Spain was neither a reliable nor a tremendously profitable trading partner and the more Puerto Rico moved away from her dependence on the mother country, the faster her economy would develop.

<u>Right</u>, slave market in Puerto Rico.

In 1820 the population of Puerto Rico was estimated at 150,000. By 1900 it had mushroomed to almost a million. The character of society drastically changed; for the first time, agitators for Puerto Rican autonomy were vocal and posed a serious threat to the Spanish government. Increasingly, the royally appointed governor and army would be identified as an impediment to the achievement of Puerto Rican independence. In 1820 Pedro Dubois had scarcely initiated a recruitment program when he was discovered by the government. The governor incarcerated Dubois at El Morro and had him executed before a firing squad.

Three years after the Dubois incident, another event in the struggle for autonomy took place. After the restoration of Ferdinand to the throne in 1814, a series of governors with absolute power ruled Puerto Rico. On the first day of 1820, an army commander declared the liberal reformist constitution of 1812 to be still in effect. One by one officials of various districts joined him. The already weak king, hoping to avoid an all-out revolution, had to concede, and called for a meeting of the *Cortes* for the first time in a decade. Jose María Quiñones went as the representative from Puerto Rico in 1823. He submitted a plan to introduce more autonomy to the island colonies, particularly in the administration of domestic affairs. The *Cortes* approved the Quiñones proposal, but their intentions fell to pieces before they could see them through. In 1823 the constitutional government of Spain collapsed. The king returned to absolute power and appointed the first of 14 governors of Puerto Rico who exercised unlimited authority over the colony, collectively staging a 42-year reign of oppression and virtual martial law.

The first of these dictators was Miguel de la Torre. Hanging on to the governorship for 15 years, Torre imposed a 10 o'clock curfew and established the *visita* – an islandwide inspection network that allowed him to keep abreast of activity in the colony and maintain tight security. Although Torres's reign was oppressive, it had some benefits.

Left, battling in the Spanish-American War.

He took control of the country's development, built roads and bridges and brought in huge numbers of black slaves to foster sugar production, contributing significantly to the lasting development of the local economy.

Subversive beards: In 1838 a group of separatists led by Buenaventura Quiñones plotted a putsch. Word of the conspiracy leaked out and several of the participants were executed; the others were exiled. Declaring beards subversive, the new governor banned the wearing of facial hair. Subsequent governors passed laws aimed at the suppression of blacks (following the historic slave rebellion on Martinique) and instituted the *libreta* laws which required all inhabitants of Puerto Rico to carry passbooks and restricted unauthorized movement. It was a troubled time for the beautiful island: between 1848 and 1867, seven consecutive military dictators governed the island, taking advantage of the institutions put into place by the Torres administration. To add to the colony's misery, in the 1850s a cholera epidemic swept across the island, claiming the lives of 30,000. Ramón Emeterio Betances, a doctor renowned for his efforts against the epidemic, was exiled in 1856 for his criticism of the colonial authorities.

Intimidated by growing separatist fervor in Puerto Rico and Cuba and by the Dominican Revolution in 1862, the crown of Spain invited Puerto Rico and Cuba in 1865 to draft a colonial constitution in the form of a "Special Law of the Indies." The documents which emerged called for the abolition of slavery, for freedom of the press and speech, and for independence on a Commonwealth basis. While the crown dragged its feet in granting these concessions, in Puerto Rico the angry governor, José María Marchessi, exiled several leading reformists, including the recently returned Betances. Fleeing to New York, they joined with other separatist Puerto Ricans and Cubans.

From New York the autonomists directed the independence movement during the 1860s and 1870s under the aegis of the Puerto Rican Revolutionary Committee. Covert satellite organizations formed in villages and towns across Puerto Rico, centering around

Mayagüez. On September 23, 1868, several hundred men congregated at a farm outside the northwestern mountain town of Lares. Marching under a banner that read *Libertad o Muerte. Viva Puerto Rico Libre. Año 1868* ("Liberty or Death. Long Live Free Puerto Rico. Year 1868") they took the town and arrested its officials. They elected a provisional president and proclaimed the Republic of Puerto Rico. The Republic would be short-lived. Troops sent by the governor met inclined toward joining the ambitious Spanish Republicans and remaining a semi-autonomist colony under the new Republic of Spain. And the most moderate of separatists thought that fusion with the Spanish Liberal Party would create a viable relationship with Spain. They believed that a monarch installed by the Liberals would grant Puerto Rico independence without the violence and hostility of a revolution. At the other end of the spectrum were the Conservatives who

the rebel front at San Sebastián and won an easy victory. Within six weeks the echoes of the *Grito de Lares* – "the Shout of Lares" – had died completely, although it has retained lasting symbolic importance in the Puerto Rican independence movement.

A short-lived Republican government in Spain instituted some reforms but these were undone by a coup in 1875. Hard-core autonomists wanted to cleave completely the colony's ties with Spain. Other separatists felt that any talk of separatism was treason. In general, members of the middle-class and peasants fell in the autonomist camp while the wealthy planters and landowners were Conservative. But many Puerto Ricans were Conservative simply because they feared – not without grounds – that if the colony separated from Spain it would be taken over by the more alien and frighteningly aggressive United States.

When the Puerto Rican Liberals gathered

in Ponce to demand autonomy combined with union with Spain, the alarmed Conservatives sent a desperate petition to the king begging him to send a new governor general. Soon the new appointee, Romualdo Palacio González, arrived. He more than satisfied the Conservatives' demands. Demonstrating an almost paranoid fear of subversive activity, he administered cruel punishment to those he considered threatening to the state. Hundreds of people were tortured

became Spain's ruler and he immediately declared Puerto Rico an autonomist state.

Adopting a two-chamber constitutional republican form of government, Sagasta's pact elected a lower house of assembly and half of the delegates to the upper house. The governor was still appointed by Spain, but his power was carefully restricted. The new government assumed power in July 1898. Later that month General Nelson A. Miles of the United States landed on the southern

to death during the "year of terror."

Brief independence: Puerto Rico did enjoy a brief flash of autonomy in 1897. The Autonomist Party voted to fuse with the monarchic Liberal Party of Spain after forming a pact with their leader Mateo Sagasta which guaranteed Puerto Rican autonomy if the Liberals came to power. On the assassination of the Spanish prime minister, Sagasta

Above, 19th-century Spanish currency.

coast with an army of 16,000 men. It was the beginning of the Spanish-American War and the end of short-lived Puerto Rican autonomy.

The US steps in: "It wasn't much of a war, but it was all the war there was," Teddy Roosevelt reflected on the Spanish-American War. On August 31, 1898, Spain surrendered. The Puerto Rico campaign had lasted only two weeks, the whole war less than four months. The United States was at the height of its imperial power under the McKinley administration. Unlike Cuba, which gained autonomy in 1898, Puerto Rico did not have the necessary native army to prevent America's annexation of the island as a protectorate. General Miles tried to assuage the inhabitants' anxiety, however, telling them, "We have come… to promote your prosperity and to bestow upon you the immunities and blessing of the liberal institutions of our government." His assurances did not pacify everyone. Ramón Emeterio Betances, now aging, issued a warning to his fellow Puerto Ricans: "If Puerto Rico does not act fast, it will be an American colony forever."

On December 10, 1898, the Treaty of Paris which settled the final terms of Spain's surrender was signed. In addition to a large reparations payment, the United States won Puerto Rico and the Philippines from Spain, but Puerto Rico wasn't exactly a grand prize at the time. Her population had reached a million. A third were blacks and mulattoes who generally possessed a little capital or land. Only an eighth of the population was literate, and only one out of 14 of the island's 300,000 children was in school. Two percent of the population owned more than two-thirds of the agricultural land. Yet 60 percent of the land owned was mortgaged at high interest rates.

It ain't over till it's over: The United States set up a military government and Puerto Rico was placed under the charge of the War Department. Assuming a hard-headed approach to the problem of underdevelopment and a lagging economy, the first three governors-general enjoyed almost dictatorial power. They introduced American currency, suspended defaulted mortgages and promoted trade with the United States. They improved public health, reformed tax laws, and overhauled local government. But the Puerto Rican people were still unhappy.

The autonomy they were on the brink of achieving when war erupted was as vital to them now as ever. Yet their new conquerors were reluctant to give any ground in the struggle for home rule.

A leading autonomist leader, Luís Muñoz Rivera, organized a new party in an attempt to reach a compromise between the separatists and the United States government. The Federal Party and its ally, the new Republican Party, advocated cooperation with the United States, especially in commercial matters, full civil rights and an autonomous civilian government. But not even the conciliatory approach Muñoz endorsed satisfied the McKinley administration. The colonial governor-general George W. Davis reported to the President that "the people generally have no conception of political rights combined with political responsibilities." However, Puerto Ricans did show some awareness of political responsibility in the municipal election of 1899. The election, which went on for a year because of the complicated voting requirements by which only literate men over the age of 21 could vote, ended in victory for the Federals and the Republicans. In municipal elections they

BETANCES.

took control of no fewer than 66 towns.

As if political turmoil were not enough, Mother Nature interfered in the form of Hurricane San Ciriaco in 1899. Three thousand people lost their lives and the damage to property was immense. The hurricane devastated the vital sugar and coffee crops and left a fourth of the island's inhabitants without homes. The US Congress waited months before responding and finally awarded a pittance of $200,000 to the island in relief payments.

Puerto Rico faced an unhappy future. The economy was on the brink of collapse, the hostilities continued with inept American administrators, and there were the ostensibly insurmountable difficulties of illiteracy and poverty. The Secretary of War, Elihu Root, recognized the military government's inadequacy. In 1900 he proposed a program for the gradual introduction of autonomy for Puerto Ricans which President McKinley endorsed. However, though Puerto Rico was suddenly closer to autonomy than it had been since before the Spanish-American War, the path to home rule was not clear yet.

The big debate: For the next 48 years, Puerto Rico and the US had a strange colonial-protectorate relationship. While it was widely acknowledged that America possessed enormous wealth from which the colony stood to

benefit, Puerto Ricans also feared that Betances' prediction would come true – that Puerto Rico would be swallowed up culturally and economically if her bonds with the United States were to strengthen. The history of the former Spanish outpost in the 20th century has been defined by the struggle to maintain an independent identity under the pressures of American imperialism.

Puerto Rico figures prominently in recent American history. It was the first non-continental US territory and served as the test case

Left, Dr Ramón Betances spoke out against the Americans. **Above**, old soldier in San Cristóbal.

for the formation and implementation of colonial policy.

Special interest groups in the United States polarized into two lobbies. The agricultural contingent, fearing competition from Puerto Rican producers where labor costs ran lower, allied with racists who dreaded the influx of the "Latin race" which would result from granting American citizenship to Puerto Ricans. And as proof of Benjamin Franklin's observation that politics makes strange bedfellows, these opponents of the administration's Puerto Rican colonial plan found themselves under the blankets with liberal Democrats who opposed imperialism of any sort.

Ever since the mid-19th century, Americans had been instructed to heed their "manifest destiny" and had settled in the west and in Alaska. Before 1900, the seeds of expansionism had blossomed into an imperialism that led some politicians to suggest annexing Mexico and Central America with hopes of eventually spreading out into the whole hemisphere. The heirs to this tradition, for the most part Republicans, sided with President McKinley on the Puerto Rico question.

The burgeoning of a colony: With the passage of the Foraker Act in 1900, Puerto Rico took on a new colonial status. A presidentially appointed governor, an Executive Council comprising both Americans and Puerto Ricans, and a House of Delegates would perform the functions of government.

In addition, a Resident Commissioner chosen by the Puerto Rican people would speak for the colony in the House of Representatives, but would have no vote. An initial 15-percent tariff was imposed on all imports to and exports from the United States and the revenues would be used to benefit Puerto Rico. After two years, free trade was promised. The colonial government would determine its own taxation programs and oversee the insular treasury. Ownership of large estates by American corporations was discouraged, at least in intention, by the prohibition of businesses from carrying on agriculture on more than 500 acres. However, officials rarely enforced this clause and capital-rich firms from the United States moved in.

Reception of the Foraker Act could have been better. An immediate challenge to its constitutional legality brought it before the Supreme Court of the United States where the majority declared that constitutionality was not applicable in an "unincorporated entity" like Puerto Rico. Dissenting Chief Justice Fuller wrote that it left Puerto Rico "a disembodied shade in an intermediate state of ambiguous existence." Repeatedly the independence factions demanded that Congress hold an insular plebiscite to let the inhabitants determine the island's future. Soon the anti-American politicians held a majority among the elected officials. As a protest against US policy, they refused to pass any legislation during 1909. They sent a submission to the president and Congress in which they claimed that it was "impossible for the people's representatives to pass the laws they desire," under the Foraker Act.

The Jones-Shafroth Act affronted many Puerto Rican statesmen. For years they had pressed for a break from the US and now, in blatant contradiction of their demands, Congress was drawing them in even more. Muñoz Rivera, the Resident Commissioner, had beseeched Congress to hold a plebiscite – but to no avail. The "Catch-22" of Puerto Rico's relationship with the US had emerged full-blown. The more political maturity the colony showed, the more fervently nationalists agitated for independence. The more hostile to the US the colony seemed to American lawmakers, the more reluctant they were to give any ground. As the House Insular Affairs Committee chairman admonished the House

The Congress responded by approving the previous year's budget in lieu of a new one. The fight for independence raged on.

Reluctant US citizens: On the eve of America's entry into World War I in 1917, President Wilson approved the Jones-Shafroth Act granting US citizenship to all Puerto Ricans. Under a clause in the new law, those who objected to becoming US citizens could defer it by signing an official document. About 200 Puerto Ricans did just that, providing inspiration to a group of like-minded *independentistas* who, in late 1933, renounced their US citizenship and issued themselves symbolic Puerto Rican passports.

of Delegates in 1920: "There is a legitimate ground for a larger measure of self-government, but that has been greatly injured by independence propaganda." The independence advocates needed a new tactic.

During this period of antagonism between Puerto Rico and the US, the economy and the population grew rapidly. Efforts to combat poor health care and disease had resulted in a precipitous drop in the death rate. Meanwhile, employment increased, production skyrocketed, and government revenues rose. Big US corporations pocketed most of the profits from this growth, and their sway with Congress assured them continued wealth.

The average Puerto Rican family earned between $150 and $200 a year; many *jíbaros* had sold their own little farms to work for American farm estates and factories.

Pablo Iglesias, a disciple of Samuel Gompers, one of the fathers of American trade unions, led the move to organize Puerto Rican laborers. At first the government opposed his efforts and his persistence landed him in jail. An appeal from the American Federation of Labor won his release, but the hostility remained. Ever a believer in compromise and change from within the system, Gompers toured Puerto Rico in 1904 in hopes of pacifying both sides. An inspection of factories and plantations, however, filled

him with disgust for his country's policies which facilitated such drastic social inequity and poor working conditions.

By 1909 the labor movement, organized under Iglesias' leadership as the Free Federation, identified itself with the labor union movement in the US. They even assumed the task of Americanizing Puerto Rico. "The labor movement in Porto Rico," Iglesias wrote, "has no doubt been, and is, the most efficient and safest way of conveying the sentiments and feelings of the American

<u>Left</u>, American medical officers at Coamo Springs. <u>Above</u>, the Puerto Rican national crest.

people to the hearts of the people of Porto Rico." A 1914 cigar strike and a 1915 cane strike brought publicity. Iglesias was elected to the new Senate of Puerto Rico in 1917.

Trouble shooting: The Great Depression of the 1930s nearly undid Puerto Rico. Two hurricanes accompanied the collapse of the economy – San Felipe in 1928 and San Cipriano in 1932 – destroying millions of dollars' worth of property and crops. Starvation and disease took a heavy toll on the population during the Depression. Across the island, haggard, demoralized people waited in long queues for inadequate government food handouts. But out of the poverty and deprivation, a new voice emerged.

It belonged to Pedro Albizu Campos, a former US Army officer and a graduate of Harvard Law School. He was of a generation of Puerto Ricans who were children at the time of the United States' takeover. Equipped with a great understanding of the American system, he used it to become a leader of militant revolutionaries. Albizu's accusation was (according to American foreign policy and international law) that the United States' claims on Puerto Rico were illegal since Puerto Rico was already autonomous at the time of occupation.

The strength and seriousness of Albizu's Nationalist organization were made clear on February 23, 1936. Two of his followers, Hiram Rosado and Elías Beauchamp, shot and killed the chief of police of San Juan. The assassins were arrested and summarily beaten to death, and Albizu and seven key party members were imprisoned in the Federal Prison in Georgia.

A year later, however, the party was still strong. Denied a permit to hold a demonstration in the town of Ponce, a group of Albizu's followers dressed in black shirts assembled to march on March 21, 1937. As the procession moved forward to the tune of *La Borinqueña* – the Puerto Rican anthem – a shot rang out. The origin of the gunfire has never been determined, but within moments both the police and the marchers were exchanging bullets. Twenty people were killed and another hundred wounded in the panic-stricken crossfire that subsequently ensued. The Governor called the affair "a riot;" the American Civil Liberties Union labeled it "a massacre." The event is still remembered today as *La Massacre de Ponce*.

The United States began to export Puerto Rico's share of the New Deal in 1933, but it was not a winning hand. President Franklin Roosevelt sent a string of inept appointments to the Governor's Mansion in San Juan, and their attempts to provide relief proved inadequate and aggravating to the Puerto Ricans. Then, from amidst the crumbling political parties, a brilliant star in Puerto Rico's history appeared. Luís Muñoz Marín, son of the celebrated statesman Luís Muñoz Rivera, had served in government since 1932 and had used his charm and connections with the American political elite to bring attention to the plight of the colony. In 1938, young Muñoz Marín founded the Popular Democratic Party, running on the slogan "Bread, Land and Liberty," and adopting the *pava* – the broad-brimmed straw hat worn by *jíbaros* – as the party symbol. In 1940, the *populares* took over half the total seats in the upper and lower Houses.

Muñoz Marín, elected leader of the Senate, decided to try to work with the new governor to achieve recovery. The appointee, Rexford Guy Tugwell, was refreshingly different from his predecessors. Able to speak Spanish and evincing a genuine compassion for the Puerto Ricans, he seemed promising. Muñoz Marín's good faith paid off. By improving the distribution of relief resources and by proposing a plan for long-term economic development contingent upon continued union with the United States, Muñoz Marín convinced Tugwell that Puerto Rico was finally ready to assume the responsibility of electing its own governor.

First popular governor: As a first step, President Roosevelt appointed Puerto Rico's resident commissioner, Jesús Piñero, to the post. In 1946 Piñero became the first native governor in the island's history. The cautious progress did not placate everyone, however, The *independentistas* accused Muñoz Marín of needlessly selling out to the United States and petitioned the United Nations for help in shaking off colonial status. Simultaneously, the United States unveiled plans for the popu-

Left, industry (here a rum distillery) is supported by US legislation. **Right**, Uncle Sam's daughter.

lar election of Puerto Rico's governor, showing new confidence in the colony.

The people elected Muñoz Marín, of course. In 1948 he took office as the first popularly elected governor and put forth his proposal for turning Puerto Rico into an *Estado Libre Asociado* – an associated free state. Learning from the newly independent Philippines, where instant autonomy had crippled economic and social progress, the US delayed endorsing Muñoz Marín's plan. However, in 1950, President Truman ap-

proved Public Law 600, the Puerto Rican Commonwealth Bill. It provided for a plebiscite in which voters would decide whether to remain a colony or assume status as a commonwealth. As the latter, Puerto Ricans would draft their own constitution, though the US Congress would retain "paramount power." In June 1951, Puerto Rico voted three to one in favor of the commonwealth.

Two disturbing events punctuated the otherwise smooth transition to commonwealth status. On the very day President Truman signed Public Law 600, a group of armed Nationalists marched on the Governor's Mansion, La Fortaleza. In a brief skirmish a policeman and four Nationalists were gunned down. Simultaneously, outbursts in five other towns including Ponce and Arecibo left over a hundred casualties, including 27 dead. The violence extended beyond Puerto Rican shores. Two Puerto Ricans from New York traveled to Washington and made an attempt on the president's life a month later. In March 1954, four Puerto Rican Nationalists, shouting "*¡Viva Puerto Rico Libre!*" fired into the House of Representatives from the visitors' gallery, wounding five Congressmen.

Muñoz Marín resigned from political office in 1964 but his party remained in power. In 1966 a commission determined that commonwealth, statehood and independence all deserved consideration. Seven months later crops left Puerto Rico subject to too many risks: weather, foreign production and interest rates. The government established the Puerto Rican Industrial Development Corporation in 1942 to oversee the development of government-sponsored manufacturing. When the state plans floundered, the administration cancelled the program and initiated a new plan, known as Operation Bootstrap.

Aimed at developing an economy based on rum, tourism and industry, the program sent dozens of public relations agents to the mainland on promotional tours. A massive advertising campaign extolled the virtues of the Puerto Rican climate, geography, economy and people in the mass media. During the early years of Operation Bootstrap, jobs

the PDP, pushing for a decision, passed a bill mandating a plebiscite. Muñoz re-entered the fray in support of continuing as a commonwealth. He argued that Puerto Rico had placed fourth in the worldwide rate of economic progress only due to its relationship with the US. Further, he claimed, statehood could easily bring an end to the independent culture of Puerto Rico. His arguments held sway: two-thirds of the ballots in 1967 were cast for Muñoz Marín's commonwealth.

Muñoz Marín had long ago recognized that the key to averting future economic catastrophe lay in avoiding a dependence on agriculture. Relying heavily on one or two in manufacturing quadrupled to over 20,000 and between 1950 and 1954 over 100,000 Puerto Ricans moved to the mainland in order to take advantage of the wartime labor market. In New York they became the archetypal Latinos, later celebrated in Bernstein's *West Side Story*, starring the Puerto Rican actress Rita Moreno A slowdown followed the resumption of peace, but in 1955, manufacturing contributed more to the economy than agriculture for the first time ever.

Tax holiday: Operation Bootstrap later evolved into Section 936, a clause in the US

<u>Above</u>, Rita Moreno in *West Side Story*.

48

DRUG COUNTRY

Mention Caribbean drug exports, and people are likely to think of *ganja* being smuggled out on leaky boats, or vials of cocaine tucked into airplane carry-on luggage. In Puerto Rico, however, drugmaking generally means the manufacturing of pharmaceuticals – the legal kind – for large-scale shipment to the United States and other countries.

Drugs, in fact, are very big business here. Some $6 billion worth of medications are produced and exported every year, making pharmaceuticals the island's most important industry and accounting for more than a quarter of its gross domestic product. More than 100 drug companies have plants in Puerto Rico, including just about every pharmaceutical firm on the Fortune 500 list. And they churn out thousands of different products, from Anacin (for headache relief) to Zantac (an over-the-counter ulcer medication).

In addition, a dizzying variety of prescription tranquilizers, anti-hypertensives, cardiovascular drugs and birth-control pills also carry the "Made in Puerto Rico" label.

All are manufactured here because of Section 936, a job-creating clause of the United States Internal Revenue Code. In a nutshell, this complicated law exempts companies from paying federal income tax on profits generated by their Puerto Rican operations.

This program has come under fire many times from US Congressmen, who say Section 936 costs American taxpayers more than $2 billion a year. Ending the program, they argue, would also punish drug companies which "gorge the public" on prescription drugs. The argument can also be made that for all the profits, only 18,000 Puerto Ricans work in the pharmaceutical industry – a number too low to justify such huge tax breaks.

Yet Section 936 remains in place, and investors don't seem to worry too much. Abbott Laboratories is spending $200 million – the largest single expansion in Puerto Rican history – to enlarge its bulk pharmaceutical operation in Barceloneta. Other companies include American Home Products Corp., Bristol-Myers Squibb Co., Eli Lily Industries and Johnson & Johnson.

Besides the drugs themselves, companies also manufacture health-care products such as intravenous solutions, blood-pressure kits and thermometers on the island. In fact, Puerto Rico's largest private employer is Baxter Healthcare Corp., which has 6,000 workers in nine factories and three service centers throughout the island.

One of the first drugmakers to set up shop here was Searle & Co., which in 1969 established a huge factory in Caguas. By the mid-1980s, the island surpassed New Jersey in United States drug production and was well on its way to becoming pharmaceutical capital of the world.

Today, modern, state-of-the-art drug factories can be found just about everywhere in Puerto Rico, even in remote mountain towns like Marcao and Jayuya. The industry seems most prevalent, however, in Carolina (a suburb of San Juan), and in the Arecibo-Barceloneta-Manatí strip along

Puerto Rico's north coast.

Hidden behind high fences, island drug factories generally have the greenest lawns anywhere, thanks to careful landscaping and rich chemical effluents in the wastewater. Their workers are well-paid, often earning $10 an hour – the highest average manufacturing wage of any industry in Puerto Rico.

Some towns are now almost entirely dependent on these companies – and on the jobs and business which they generate. In the town of Humacao, for example, Medtronic of Minneapolis assembles pacemakers, Sandoz of Switzerland makes Ex-Lax and Syntex of Panama produces birth-control pills – all within 10 minutes of each other. ■

Right, pharmaceutical production in Caguas.

Internal Revenue Code that since the mid-1970s has exempted manufacturers from paying federal income tax on profits earned by their subsidiaries in Puerto Rico. Thanks to 936, some 2,000 factories now operate throughout the island churning out everything from Microsoft floppy disks to Starkist tuna, all for the huge American market.

The future of this controversial tax holiday is perennially in doubt. Opponents say Section 936 costs the US taxpayer more than $2 billion a year while doing little to relieve unemployment in Puerto Rico. Backers point to the 300,000 direct and indirect manufacturing jobs 936 has created and plead with Congress not to abolish the incentives.

In 1985, when Section 936 was threatened by Congressional budget-cutters, former governor Rafael Hernández Colón came up with a novel approach to save it: he offered to link 936 to President Reagan's Caribbean Basin Initiative, a trade program designed to help the struggling economies of Central America and the Caribbean, As a result of the deal 936 was rescued, and Puerto Rico agreed to fund at least $100 million worth of development projects a year in selected CBI beneficiary nations. Puerto Rico's Economic Development Agency (known locally as Fomento) claims that in the following decade $1 billion in so-called "936 funds" financed more than 150 projects in the Caribbean, creating 35,000 jobs in Puerto Rico and neighboring islands.

US subsidies and direct manufacturing investment have given Puerto Rico a per-capita income of around $6,300. Though this is far less than the poorest US state, Mississippi, it tops most other Caribbean islands and outranks anywhere in Latin America.

Prosperity is measured in other ways. Virtually every Puerto Rican family owns a TV set; nearly all enjoy telephone services; and there are 1½ million cars on the island, nearly one for every two inhabitants. Fuel consumption is half the total of the Caribbean.

On the other hand, Puerto Rico is plagued with overpopulation, water contamination, deforestation, a high Aids rate and a frightening number of crimes. Around 800 murders are committed every year, making it one of the most violent places in the Caribbean outside of Haiti. Sociologists blame many of the problems on the identity crisis caused by Puerto Rico's unsure political status.

Under Commonwealth status, Puerto Ricans are exempt from US federal income tax, though they do pay personal income taxes to their own government and are subjected to US army draft. More Puerto Ricans died in Vietnam per capita than soldiers from any US state – all having been sent there by a president for whom they could not vote. In 1986 a Puerto Rican pilot was shot down in an air raid against Libya's Colonel Qadaffi. In 1993 the first casualty in Somalia was Puerto Rican.

Because Puerto Rico is not an independent nation, there is no Puerto Rican passport and travel to the US mainland is unrestricted. Some 2½ million now live in *los estados*, about half of them in New York City.

Although island residents cannot vote in US presidential elections, they can vote in the Democratic and Republican primaries, which is why presidential candidates sometimes campaign here. Puerto Ricans also elect a resident commissioner to the US House of Representatives who has a voice but no vote on legislative matters.

Two parties are fighting to change that. The Partido Nuevo Progressivo (PNP), founded in 1968, wants to make Puerto Rico the 51st state. This, the party claims, would rapidly give the island economic parity with the rest of the US, though it wants to keep sufficient sovereignty to participate separately in the Olympics and the Miss Universe contest. But a plebiscite in 1993 showed a narrow majority opposed to statehood, with the majority preferring the status quo.

At the other end of the spectrum is the Partido Independentista Puertorriqueño (PIP). Along with a much smaller faction headed by the socialists, the PIP dreams of a republic free of US influence. These *independentistas* make lots of headlines but rarely win more than 5 percent of the island votes.

The third party, the Partido Democratico Popular (PDP), favors continued Commonwealth status and sees both statehood and independence as potential economic and social disasters. The party's description of the Commonwealth could, perhaps, apply to the state of Puerto Rico in general: "*Lo mejor de dos mundos*" – the best of both worlds.

Right, the island's relationship with the United States stirs up strong – and mixed – emotions, which emerge in political rallies.

There is a song, one among many, which stands as the most evocative of what it means to live in the paradise which is Puerto Rico. If not in fact – there is squalor amid the great natural beauty, a certain sadness amid the promise – this paradise exists in the heart.

Written by José Manuel Rivera, "Mi Tierra Borincana" extols with deceptive simplicity the reasons to endure the *tapones* (traffic jams) in San Juan, the ineptitude of certain bureaucracies, and even the preciousness of certain resources – water in particular – which Continentals (non-Puerto Ricans from the mainland who come to live here) too often take for granted or with impatience.

"How beautiful it is, to live in this dreamland! And how beautiful it is to be the master of the *coquí's* song!" as the song says. "What an advantage it is to reap the coffee of this great gift!"

In a certain sense, the lyrics are themselves an illusion, yet in another they're very real. For while life on the island for natives and emigrants alike is not what it was 20 or even 10 years ago – there is more crime in the bigger cities; its working class works harder for what seems to be less and less – its lure, for those who truly love Puerto Rico, is not diminished.

Living anywhere within the Commonwealth requires a balance of cleverness, common sense, and hard realism for Puerto Ricans and Continentals alike. Opulence is hardly uncommon among those who can afford it – in the wealthier suburbs of San Juan, for example, a modest-looking three-bedroom house with a small yard can cost upwards of $200,000 – but even so the display of wealth isn't encouraged.

Sense of pleasure: What's more important is a sense of belonging, acquired largely through willing readjustment to Puerto Rico's pace. The practice of businesses closing from noon until two or even three in the afternoon isn't as prevalent as it used to be, due mostly to the increasing use of air-conditioning, but it is not uncommon. And the attitude behind it is

Preceding pages: on the way to the fiesta, Ponce; relaxing on Culebra Island. **Left**, street party in the San Sebastián Festival.

certainly quite a healthy one. It's an attitude which sees work not as an end in itself, but a means to fund subsequent enjoyment.

Weekends are taken very seriously, and major holidays, especially Christmas, even more so. In the States, Christmas lasts perhaps a week; on the island the celebrations begin in mid-December and don't stop until Three Kings' Day, January 6. It's presumed by residents that there will be company, people coming from far away to visit or just neighbors stopping by from roughly December 15 (also the official start of the tourist season, which ends on April 15 of the following year) until the last *pasteles* (tamales) are eaten and the last glasses of *coquíto* (egg nog with rum) consumed.

Though the University of Puerto Rico's ambitious School of Agriculture continues to experiment with ways of growing the kinds of produce which now have to be imported, fruits and vegetables which are almost ubiquitously common in the States are usually hard to find.

Local produce: And yet, who needs apples when there are still trucks along almost every major road selling native oranges – *chinas* (chee-nas) – at a few dollars for a big bag? Despite the incursion of a horde of mainland products of dubious nutritional repute – the Puerto Rican sweet tooth matches that of the Italians and the Viennese – *comida Criolla* is still the food of the day in most households.

It's heavy food, rich with an invigorating assortment of beans, from *arroz con habichuelas* (rice with either small pink beans or kidney beans) and *arroz con gandules* (pigeon peas) to *lechón asado* (whole roast suckling pig) prepared almost exclusively for holidays and large family gatherings, and its counterpart, *perníl* (fresh picnic ham in most Stateside butcher shops and supermarkets). Both are seasoned with *adóbo*, a thick, fragrant paste of garlic, vinegar, peppercorns, and parsley or oregano.

Strangely, for a place with so much marine bounty – its waters are full of grouper, yellowtail, spiny lobster, squid, sea snail, conch and shark – native Puerto Ricans shun fish, preferring chicken and pork. Salt cod – *bacalao* – is, however, a staple.

Siestas, cars and crime: With or without the

Right, the hat is local, but the blond hair and blue eyes are a Continental legacy.

benefits of a *siesta*, quality eating, still done mostly during the lunch hour, tends to make the pace of transacting business a little slower; even, perhaps, more sensible. Only behind the wheels of the island's 1½ million cars – Puerto Rico ranks sixth in the world for the ratio of motor vehicles to people – is there any indication that anyone is in a hurry.

Automobiles are bought for either practicality or show, and those who buy for show know they're taking risks. Gasoline is more expensive here than on the US mainland, and the island's poverty has been a sad and consistent fact of life. It explains in part the decorative iron grillwork known as *rejas*, found on almost every middle- and upper-class home.

Sadly, violent crime, and this includes everything from carjacking to murder, plagues Puerto Rico like never before. On December 31 each year, local newspapers announce a new high in the annual homicide tally. Surveys consistently show voters are far more concerned about crime than political status or anything else. The violence is blamed largely on drugs – as is the island's severe Aids epidemic – but politicians haven't found solutions to any of those problems.

Barrios and barriers: In the meantime, wealthier Puerto Ricans are protecting themselves from crime by closing their neighborhoods to outsiders. Today, many of San Juan's best *urbanizaciones* – Parkside, Caparra Heights and Torremar, to name a few – are islands unto themselves; the streets leading to them are barricaded with electronic gates that open only to residents and approved visitors. The closed neighborhoods, unheard of 10 years ago, have sparked debates over the legality of such practices. Until the crime rate comes down, however, they are sure to continue.

Puerto Rico's ills may also be attributed to sheer overpopulation. Because of traditionally high birth rates and medical advances that caused the death rate to plummet shortly after the Spanish-American War, Puerto Rico's population jumped to over one million by 1900, and now stands at around 3.8 million. This gives the island a population density of nearly 1,100 per square mile, among the world's highest. Only Bangladesh, The Maldives, Barbados, Taiwan, South

Right, Isabelan unicyclists in a festival parade.

Korea and the city-states of Hong Kong and Singapore are more crowded. Indeed, if it weren't for the safety valve that allows Puerto Ricans unrestricted travel to the American mainland, the island might have 5 million people today.

For administrative purposes, Puerto Rico is divided into 78 municipalities. They range in size from Arecibo and Ponce, with more than 100 sq. miles, to 6 sq.-mile Cataño, home of the Bacardî rum distillery. Population-wise, the large *municipio* is San Juan, with more than 430,000 people, the smallest is offshore Culebra, with only 2,000. The island adheres half-heartedly to the metric system, which means that all distances are posted in kilometers, and gasoline is sold by the liter. Nevertheless, temperatures are still given in Fahrenheit rather than Celsius, and speed-limit signs are still in miles per hour (in order to accommodate the speedometers of American-made cars). This is unlikely to change as long as Puerto Rico remains under the US flag.

Español sî, inglés no!: A far more contentious issue is the language debate. For 90 years, the island had two official languages, Spanish and English. Then in 1991, former Governor Rafael Hernández Colón – citing Puerto Rico's "cultural heritage" – abolished English as an official language. This won him Spain's Prince of Asturias award and praise from the *independentistas*, but sparked an outcry from many local educators and business men. The controversy heated up further when Hernández Colón's pro-statehood successor, Pedro Rosselló, took office in January 1993. One of the first things he did was restore English's offical status, making Puerto Rico once again bilingual.

Regardless of the law, less than a fourth of Puerto Ricans are completely bilingual; outside the big cities, however, you will definitely need a few basic words of Spanish to get around.

Puerto Rico is a place of which it can truly be said everyone comes from somewhere else. There are the traces of Taíno and Carib blood left in the fine, high cheekbones of many of those who've lived on the island for generations and caught in the depth of their deep and beautiful eyes. In the town of Loíza in fact, the evidence of the island's slave-

<u>Right</u>, relaxing in Loíza.

trading days is impossible to ignore. There are women with skin the color of *café con leche* – the strong coffee with hot milk which is a staple on every breakfast table – whose tightly curly hair is naturally auburn, and children with liquid blue eyes and blond hair whose faces are exotically beautiful, thanks to any number of forebears – traders, pirates, artisans, slaves and colonists.

Patriotism: Despite all varieties of political differences, pride is universal and strong. Though US flags fly alongside all Puerto Rico flags in public places and schoolchildren sing "The Star Spangled Banner" before they sing "La Borinqueña," the island's own beautiful anthem, being Puerto Rican always comes first. This isn't without its paradoxical side. The people who've chosen to live here, Puerto Ricans and Continentals alike, love the island intensely, yet know that many things are far from perfect. That's where the patience, cleverness and common sense comes in.

The Ports Authority (Autoridad de Puertos), for example, is the only municipal agency which consistently makes a profit. Yet those who rely on the ferries it operates between Fajardo, Vieques and Culebra have a well-honed sense of humor towards its less-than-pristine equipment. It might take two hours. It might take six. *Así es la vida.* That's life.

There is, however, determination beneath that patience. The attitude of many towards the US Navy, which maintains a major base at Sabana Seca and conducts maneuvers in and around the island's waters, ranges from conspicuously faint affection to undisguised resentment. This was especially acute in 1970, when Culebrans were kept off Flamenco – as they had been for decades – during practice bombing runs.

"Enough," said 2,000 people all at once. The red flag went up to keep people off the beach; most of the population headed straight for it, loaded with picnic coolers. They were going to picnic until the Navy stopped their target runs so close to their beach. Three years later, the Navy finally agreed to leave Flamenco alone.

Continentals who relocate to the bigger cities and their environs learn very quickly

Left, horseback riding is a popular pastime on an island full of battered automobiles.

from their neighbors how to be practical. It's unwise, and downright foolish in some places, to flaunt wealth with fancy cars and grand houses filled with expensive possessions. To grow too attached to property is almost to court losing it.

As a result, and in no small way a fortunate one, what the island's residents really cherish are the things which have no price tags: family, friends and the pleasure, challenging as it can be, of living here.

Its anthem expresses it best. Unlike other nations' songs, which speak glowingly of military might and triumph over adversaries, "La Borinqueña" is a celebration of a reality which is at the same time an ideal:

The land of Borinquen,
where I was born
is a flowering garden
of exquisite magic.

A sky, always clear,
serves as its canopy,
and sings calm lullabies
to the waves at its feet.

When Columbus came
to its beaches,
he exclaimed full of admiration
"Oh! Oh! Oh!"

This is the beautiful land
I've been looking for;
it's Borinquen, the daughter,
the daughter of the sea and the sun,
the sea and the sun.

Puerto Rico is a place where beauty co-exists in places with squalor, a place where politics and poetry very often merge; a place where its most celebrated leaders, among them Luís Llorens Torres and Luís Muñoz Marín, were also poets.

There is poverty, certainly, a chronic ache to those who love their island. But art flourishes here too, with the craftworkers, the musicians, the composers, the playwrights and painters and sculptors and actors. It gives Puerto Rico's beauty a face which is proud yet edged in sadness, exotic yet utterly recognizable.

Left, taking a break – a forester enjoys a breather in the El Yunque rain forest.

Even before Columbus' fleet "discovered" the island of Puerto Rico in 1493, the smallest of the Great Antilles was in a state of cultural unrest. Invading Carib tribes from South America were threatening the native Arawaks as they had many other cultures throughout the Caribbean. When the local Arawaks met the invading Caribs, what language was created? The Arawak name for the island, *Borínquen*, is still used ("*La Borinqueña*" is the Puerto Rican national anthem), and the Caribs live on in the word Caribbean. Many Puerto Rican municipalities go by their pre-Columbian names: Caguas, Arecibo, Mayagüez, Yauco, Guaynabo – to name just a few. The Arawaks feared the god *Juracán*, while we fear hurricanes. And the *hamacas* in which the early Indians slept are just as popular today under the name of hammocks.

If the Arawaks welcomed the Spaniards as a strategy to ward off the Caribs, they certainly miscalculated. Instead, a wave of Spaniards swept across the island. Eventually there came battle and disease, which obliterated the native Arawak population. Then came sex, producing the first Puerto Ricans, and the first men who could claim to speak a truly Puerto Rican Spanish. The Spanish of the earliest Puerto Ricans, like that of their modern descendants, can be said to reflect either a pronunciational sloppiness or an Arawak love of diphthongs. For example, Spanish words which end in *ado* are pronounced as if the *d* were silent. Humacao is an Arawak name, but *pescao* will get you fish anywhere on the island. A good stew is an *asopao*, but if your *fiao* (your credit) isn't good enough, you won't be served one in any restaurant.

Puerto Rico's first Africans were brought as slaves, mostly from west-central Africa. These slaves brought with them another language, *santería*; many musical instruments, including the drums; and countless customs and attitudes which have found their way into the lives of everyone. The *baquine*, a festival of mourning for the death of an infant, is a ritual of African origin, and is usually the cause of a great deal of rum, dancing and *lechón asao* (roast suckling pig). By the mid-19th century, the Africans made up a fifth of the population, and such customs penetrated Puerto Rican society.

Integration of the races has worked smoothly in Puerto Rico, and it is said that *él que no tiene dinga tiene mandinga*, a phrase which attributes some amount of African ancestry to virtually all Puerto Ricans. The Mandinga were one of the more populous of the West African tribes, brought to Puerto Rico to harvest sugar-cane, coffee and tobacco.

Sugar, coffee and tobacco farmers, black, white and *mestizo* gradually became the archetypal Puerto Rican *jíbaros*. The most famous record of the customs and speech patterns of the *jíbaro* was written by Manuel A. Alonso, a doctor whose writings fit into the Latin American literary movement known as *costumbrismo*. In 1849, his book *El Gíbaro* was published in Barcelona, and in it there are invaluable accounts of a *jíbaro* wedding, dances and cockfights, Christmas celebrations and the arrival of the magic lantern in the hills. Equally important is the portrait of mid-19th century *jíbaro* speech patterns. In Alonso's verses we can hear the *jíbaro* dialect in its purest form. He mentions foods such as *lichón asao*, *toytiyas* (tortillas) and *mavi* (a tropical fruit used in a number of drinks).

For all the eccentricities of the Puerto Rican tongue, it is important to remember that the language of the island is Spanish, albeit a Spanish heavily influenced by other nationalities, and that Puerto Rican Spanish shares many eccentricities with the Spanish of its Caribbean neighbors. One such trope is *seseo*, by which *s* sounds are muted, and sometimes disappear altogether, at the end of syllables. Thus, matches are *loh fohforoh* rather than *los fosforos* and *graciah* means thanks. *Yeismo* is another variation confusing to non-Puerto Rican speakers; this involves pronouncing the Spanish *ll* and *y* sounds as English *js*, so as to render a word like *Luquillo*, the island's most popular beach, "Look here, Joe." Let's not forget the truncation of words with terminal *e* sounds, like *noch'*. In Puerto Rico, go into a coffee shop for a cup of *café co' lech*.

The granting of United States citizenship

to Puerto Ricans in 1917 signaled the advent of English as the first Germanic language to become part of the Puerto Rican dialect. The startling result of this last infusion is Spanglish, a colloquial Spanish which may be as familiar to a North American as it is to a Spaniard. Spanglish consists not only of a shared vocabulary but also of the terse sentence construction characteristic of English. The first penetration of English into Puerto Rican Spanish seems to have come from English labels on consumer products.

Indeed, men still sit at bars nursing *un scotch* while their children look on, chewing *chicletes*. The introduction of American commerce was no less confounding in other ways. When the first American cash registers were introduced in San Juan's grocery and department stores, a whole generation stood paralyzed at checkout counters when the "No Sale" tab, marking the end of the transaction, flipped up. *No Sale* translates as "Do not leave" in Spanish.

Spanglish truly entered its heyday only with the mass migration of Puerto Ricans to the United States in the 1940s. This exodus created a generation of so-called *Neorriqueños*, or "Newyoricans" who returned to their native island with the baffling customs and speech patterns of the streets of New York. Or they would send letters home with news, and, if they had no money, they would send the letter *ciodí* (cash on delivery).

Letters to the Cordillera would have to be transported by *el trucke*. Perhaps there would be bad news, that a son had been *bosteado* by the *policías* for dealing in *los drogues*. More often it was just idle chatter, discussions of the decisions of the world *líders*, or of how a brother had won a pool game by sinking the important eight ball in the corner *poquete*.

Puerto Ricans love pool, but if Puerto Rico and the Spanglish language have an official sport, it has to be *el béisbol* or baseball. Everyone knows that Roberto Clemente (from Carolina) and Orlando Cepeda (from Santurce) were Puerto Rico's greatest hitters of *jonrones* and *dobles* (home-runs and doubles). Most Puerto Ricans would say their

Preceding pages: talking it over at El Combate.

ball-players were *wilson*, meaning "very good." Some things have remained little changed, though. Dollars are sometimes called *dolares*, but more often *pesos*. Quarters are *pesetas*, nickels *vellones*, and pennies *centavos*.

Spciy talk: Puerto Rico's beaches have been the stage for dialogs in many languages, but none are as spicy as those you'll hear on the beach at Piñones between two *playeros* when the mid-winter swells are up:

PAPO: *Oye, 'mano, que pasa?* (Hey brother, what's happening?)

RAYMOND: *Cómo estamos, broki?* (How we doin', brother?)

PAPO: *Na' mas se me estallo la tabla.* (I just cracked my surfboard.)

RAYMOND: *Qué chavienda!* (What a drag!)

PAPO: *Estuve gufeando en un tubo y fua! se me fue la tabla contra esas rocas por ahi.* (I was goofing around in a tube, when, boom! my board flies into those rocks over there.)

RAYMOND: *Ea rayo!* (Geeze!)

PAPO, observing another surfer's antics: *Qué chivo! Por poco se comió el cable.* (What luck! He almost wiped out.)

RAYMOND: *Ese tipo yo lo conozco. Es bien buena gente.* (I know him, he's a good guy.)

PAPO: *Vale. Ay, pero mira a esa jeba. Vamos a rapiar.* (Cool. Oh, will you look at this babe. Let's rap.)

RAYMOND: *Oye, guapa, ven aca un momento.* (Hey, cutey, come here a minute.)

MARTA: *No seas cafre o te rompo el coco.* (Don't be rude or I'll break your head).

PAPO: *De dónde tu eres?* (Where you from?)

MARTA: *De Guaynabo y a tí que te importa?* (Guaynabo, and what do you care?)

PAPO: *A ver si quieres pon pa' San Juan que se me rayo la tabla.* (To see if you'd like a lift to San Juan, 'cause my surfboard has cracked.)

MARTA: *Bueno, vale.* (Well, okay.)

PAPO: *Cógelo suave, Raymond.* (Take it easy, Raymond.)

Having such a rich tradition, Puerto Ricans love good conversation, and, with at least four linguistic families from which to draw, enjoy a speech at once cryptic and colorful.

Christopher Columbus brought sugarcane to the Antilles from the Canary Islands on his second voyage to the New World in 1493. In 1515, settlers planted cane on the island of Puerto Rico. Three years later, they imported African slaves to grow the cane. Demand for sugar, a relative novelty on European markets, seemed insatiable, and settlers were willing to exert tremendous effort to establish sugar plantations in the Caribbean. But sugar was not the only profitable substance produced from cane. The Spanish settlers soon discovered that the liquid by-product in the manufacture of sugar crystals – molasses – fermented naturally. They invented a method of processing this molasses into rum, symbol of the Caribbean good life.

The production process: Sugar is produced by "expressing" the juice from boiled cane by pressing, rolling, or pounding it. The juice is boiled down to a concentrated syrup, placed in vats and spun at high speed, causing crystals to form. The early mills were called *ingenios* and powered by human and animal labor. Today, machines spin the syrup at a rate of 2,200 revolutions per minute.

Removing the crystals leaves a heavy, sweet molasses. This, the early settlers observed, fermented easily when exposed to the open air – free-floating yeast spores thrive in sugar environments and produce alcohol during their culture cycle. Not satisfied with the flavor and proof of this molasses wine (which many Puerto Ricans used to enjoy as a beverage called *aguardiente* or *madilla*), the Spaniards distilled it, filtering out impurities and increasing the concentration of alcohol. Thus they created rum.

Rum took hold quickly as an important Puerto Rican export. In the first half of the 16th century its popularity grew with the increasing demand for sugar. Then a slump in the sugar industry as a result of Spain's mercantile policies led to a parallel decline in production. Decade after decade, rum claimed a smaller share of the Puerto Rican export trade. In the late 18th century, the Spanish government taxed Puerto Rican rum so heavily that it could no longer compete with foreign producers. During the reforms made by the Spanish Republic in 1812, the intro-duction of a new type of sugarcane and incentives for the development of colonial agriculture and industry fostered a resurgence in the sugar and rum markets. They limped along for 100 years, rising and falling with the tides of 19th-century politics.

In 1936, the island profited from the decision of one of Cuba's great rum scions, the Bacardí family, to move their center of production to San Juan. Today, in a computer-age facility across San Juan Bay in Cataño, Bacardí is the world's largest rum producer.

In the 1930s, a program for the development of the Puerto Rican rum industry was established under New Deal legislation. Since gaining status as an associated free state in the 1950s, Puerto Rico has included rum in all its government programs for economic development, including Operation Bootstrap.

Over the centuries, Puerto Rican rum distillers have refined their methods to produce the appealing liquid available today. Rather than depend on air-borne yeast spores, they add select cultures to guarantee consistent quality. Water and old mash from cane boiling are also added. For two to three days the mixture ferments until it is 7 percent alcohol.

Distillation in a still can bring it up as high as 160 proof. The higher the proof, the lower the congeners, the lighter the body, and the more neutral the color.

Puerto Rican rum is distinguished from the rums of other Caribbean countries by its light body and smooth flavor. A fine rum to consume neat, it possesses a subtlety which makes it a good mixer. There are three categories. White, or silver rum is year-old rum that has been leached and filtered. This pure liquid is quite dry, and only a very slight trace

Daiquiri
Boil one part water with two parts sugar for 5 minutes to make a sugar syrup.
   Mix: ½ jigger of sugar syrup
   1½ jiggers lime juice
   6 jiggers gold rum. Stir with ¾ cup crushed ice and strain over ice.
Frozen Daiquiri
Whip:
   2–3 cups crushed ice
   3 tablespoons powdered sugar
   1½ jiggers lime juice

of molasses flavor is evident. Amber, or gold rum is aged for three years. Producers add caramel to give it a rich, sunny color and mellow taste. Gold rum is usually sold at 80 proof. Liqueur rums are aged the longest, and are dry but mellow. They are sold as Red Label or Heavy Dark rum.

Puerto Rican rums are the best choice for cocktails but use the darker rums of Jamaica and Guyana for punches – the flavor of the Puerto Rican rums is too subtle.

Four popular rum-based cocontions are:

   6 jiggers rum in a blender until snowy
Hot Buttered Rum
Into a mug, pour
   1 teaspoon powdered sugar
   ¼ cup boiling water
   ¼ cup rum and stir. Flavor with a generous dash of nutmeg and a pat of butter.
Hot Rum Toddy
Into a mug, put
   1 teaspoon powdered sugar
   1 jigger rum
   1 stick cinnamon
   3 whole cloves
   ½ lemon slice.
Fill the mug with ¾ cup hot water.

Preceding pages: luscious rum concoctions. Left, rum casks, Arecibo. Above, Bacardí garden.

Carib and Spanish destruction of Puerto Rico's native Taíno tribes, for all its ruthlessness, was far from complete. It has been said that Puerto Rican society today reflects its African and Indian origins more than its Spanish ones, and there is much truth in that. Non-Spanish ways live on in customs, rituals, language and all aspects of life, and one can see in many facial features the unfamiliar expression of the Taíno, a race otherwise lost to us forever. But nowhere is the Taíno influence more visible, or more welcome, than in Puerto Rican cuisine, one of the great culinary amalgams of our hemisphere.

Imagine a Taíno man – call him Otoao and set his caste at *naboría*, one of the higher agricultural castes in the Taíno hierarchy – rising one sunny morning after having won a glorious victory the previous day over the invading Caribs. This victory was cause for an *areyto*, the ritual Taíno celebration which either preceded or followed any happening of even the remotest importance. Births, deaths, victories, defeats... it's *areyto* time. *Areytos*, like other socio-religious Taíno festivals, required intricate preparations for whatever food and drink was to be served, and as a *naboría*, Otoao was in charge of hunting and fishing for the tribe.

Not that Otoao's wife Tai had it terribly easy. As a *naboría* woman (women's caste was determined by that of their husbands), Tai was responsible for the cultivation and harvesting of the fields (*conucos*) as well as the preparation of the meals. These were elaborate, and the Taínos managed to get an astounding range of food on the banquet table. The menu that evening included roast *jutías* (early guinea pigs) seasoned with sweet red chilli peppers, fried fish in corn oil, fresh shellfish and a variety of freshly harvested vegetables. Among the vegetables were *yautías* (starchy tubers similar to potatoes and yams), corn yams, cassava and the same small red chili peppers used to season the *jutías*. Bread was *casabe*, a mixture of puréed cassava and water cooked between two hot rocks. For dessert, the Taínos had fresh fruit

Preceding pages: roasting pig. **Left**, picking green peppers. **Right**, *frituras*, a local favorite.

picked from the extensive variety available throughout the island. The culmination of the celebration was the drinking of an alcoholic beverage made from fermented corn juice. This activity was accompanied by the ceremonial inhalation of hallucinogenic fumes thought to make the warriors fitter for battle. The Taínos made hallucinogens of many sorts, the most common of which used the hanging, bell-shaped flowers of the *campana* tree to make a potent and mind-bending tea.

Most of the dietary staples mentioned above survive in the Puerto Rican cuisine of today, albeit some in altered form. Puerto Rican cooking is now an amalgam of the Taíno, the Spanish and the African traditions. Much of this interpenetration took place early in the island's history, with Spanish colonists incorporating a variety of their own ingredients and techniques into the native cuisine, most of which were found to blend surprisingly well. A tremendous addition to this culinary melange was made by the Africans brought as slaves shortly thereafter. The African tradition is responsible for what is perhaps the greatest achievement in

Caribbean cooking – the combination of strikingly contrasting flavors which in other culinary traditions would be considered unblendable. One of these savory concoctions is *piñon*, a highly popular combination which uses ripe plantains layered between well-seasoned ground beef and is almost invariably served with rice.

Food from around the world: As different ingredients and cooking techniques were introduced to the island by its early settlers, a local cooking tradition began to take shape. Most important of the early imports were the Spanish cattle, sheep, pigs, goats and other grillable creatures the islanders had never tasted and took to with zeal. Along with the

more. These products, in combination with those already present, were to mold what was to become the Puerto Rican culinary tradition. It is ironic that among these imports can be counted several for which Puerto Rico was to become renowned. Puerto Rican coffee, for example, especially that from the region around Yauco, was long considered by Europeans the best coffee one could get in the world. And the plantain, arguably the most popular staple in Puerto Rican cuisine, is something of a national symbol, almost as the leek is to the Welsh; a man who is admired for his honesty and lack of pretension is said to have on him the *mancha del plátano*, or "stain of the plantain."

animals were brought an almost infinite number of vegetables, fruits and spices from the farthest reaches of Spain's colonial empire. A subtler, but no less important, influence on the Puerto Rican food supply was the introduction of European farming methods and agricultural equipment.

Surprisingly, many of the agricultural staples which look indigenous to the island were actually brought to Puerto Rico from other parts of the world. Among the great variety of crops imported were coffee, sugarcane, coconuts, bananas, plantains, oranges and other citrus fruits, ginger and other spices, onions, potatoes, tomatoes, garlic and much

Myths and misconceptions: Puerto Rican cuisine is as eclectic as it is varied. Local food has earned a reputation it most decidedly does not deserve for being hot, fiery and spicy. In actuality, although it is prepared with a multiplicity of richly varied spices and condiments, Puerto Ricans tend to season their food more subtly than one might imagine. The base of a majority of native dishes is the *sofrito*, an aromatic and well-seasoned sauce made from puréed tomatoes, onions, garlic, green peppers, sweet red chili peppers, coriander, anatto seeds and a fairly arbitrary handful of other spices. This *sofrito* adds a zesty taste to stews, rices, stewed beans and a variety of other dishes, but only the blandest of palates would consider it to be piquant.

Native Caribbean flavors are evident in the majority of Puerto Rican recipes. The most popular dinner dishes are stewed meats, rice and beans, an enormous selection of fritters, and desserts made from local fruits and vegetables.

Social traditions of old: Puerto Ricans have very successfully kept alive not only the culinary, but also many of the social traditions of their Taíno forebears. Christmas time on the island is not complete without rice, "pigeon peas," *lechón asao* (roast suckling pig), *pasteles* (tamales made from plan-

seafood dishes tend to be accompanied by *sorrullos* (corn fritters) in most of the restaurants on the south coast from Salinas to Cabo Rojo. The same is true of the great variety of fritters available in the food shacks of Luquillo, a most rewarding 30-minute visit from San Juan for anyone interested in local cuisine. Bayamón and environs boast a truly unusual snack in *chicharrón*, a sort of massive pork-scratching sold on the highways in and out of the city. It's definitely an acquired taste, but once you've acquired it, you'll understand why there are so many hefty individuals wandering the streets.

The island offers a great variety of restaurants for tourists and local consumers. Typi-

tains and *yautías* filled with a flavorful meat stuffing) and, as dessert, a *majarete* made with rice flour, coconut milk, grated coconut pulp, sugar and spices. For the Lenten season, seafood dishes include the traditional *serenata*, codfish in a vinaigrette sauce served with tomatoes, onions, avocados and boiled vegetables.

Though Puerto Rico is far too small to have a large number of truly regional cuisines, a number of dishes are limited to particular areas of the island. For example,

<u>Left</u>, eat it on the street. <u>Above</u>, everything under the sun, ready and waiting.

cal restaurants serving local food are only rarely luxurious or expensive. In fact, among Puerto Ricans, a rule of thumb applies that the shabbier the establishment, the better the food. The best native creations are found at modest little local *fondas*, where the prices are as reasonable as the food is distinguished. In a *fonda*, you can pick up a generous plate of rice and beans, *biftec criollo* (steak), *tostones* (fried plantains), salad, a can of Medalla beer and dessert for about $8. If you can afford to splurge for the extra 30¢ you can pick up one of the better cups of coffee you will have in your life. At the low end of the economic scale are delicious sandwiches made with a mixture of red meats, cheeses, tomatoes and other ingredients. Among the most popular are *cubanos* and *media noches*. At the pricey end of the scale is *asopao*, probably Puerto Rico's most widely loved native dish. This thick stew can be made with chicken, pork or fish, and is invariably worth every penny one pays for it.

International cuisine: Besides the local restaurants, you'll find a large assortment of places in which to savor food from different continents and countries. There are Chinese, French, Spanish, Cuban, Italian, German and Mexican restaurants in the San Juan area. And if gourmet international food is not your style, rest assured that sleazy little joints

serving hamburgers, hot dogs, crispy fried chicken and other exquisite junk-food are ubiquitous throughout the island.

Making it on your own: Armchair connoisseurs who will never go to Puerto Rico and live far enough from New York City to be completely unable to procure a pre-cooked Puerto Rican delicacy will be happy to find that the stuff is fairly easy to cook – once one gets the correct ingredients – and that it provides a rewarding change-of-pace from *nouvelle cuisine*.

Here's a recipe for *mofongo*, a hearty, typically Puerto Rican plantain dish that makes a first-rate luncheon or dinner.

Mofongo abreu
Ingredients:
  3 green plantains
  ¼ cup olive oil
  1½ tsp. salt
  ½ cup grated pork rind
  2–3 cloves garlic
Cut plantains into sections like *tostones* (about 6 pieces each). Fry in corn oil until slightly browned. Drain off oil. Mix with other ingredients, using – if you want to be really Puerto Rican about the whole thing – a mortar and pestle. Shape into balls and serve in chicken stock. Chicken soup's okay, but chicken stock is the real thing. Otherwise, shape the stuff into hamburger-shaped patties and serve with *carnecita*.

Those familiar with Jewish cooking will recognize the first way of cooking *mofongo* as somewhat similar to putting matzoh balls in chicken stock. If therefore you worry that *mofongo* will be nothing new, try it with *carnecita*, which was left sufficiently vague in the preceding recipe for us to make the formula available here:

Carnecita
Ingredients:
  2 lbs. pork (the leaner the better)
  1 cup *adobo*
Cut pork into cubes about an inch square. Marinate in *adobo* 24 hours. Fry in olive oil. Serve with *mofongo*.

Yes, but as you're obviously no closer to enjoying your *mofongo*, since you probably haven't the vaguest idea of what *adobo* is, we'll give you a bit of help.

Adobo
Ingredients:
  2 cloves garlic, ground
  1½ tsps. olive oil or to taste
  ½ cup vinegar
  3 tbsp. olive oil
Stir all this up well. Slather it on the *mofongo* and forget about it for a day or so. Fry it all up, eat it, and you'll realize that *mofongo*, although it sounds like inner-city slang for "very bad person" is a tasty concoction indeed. It just might make you want to head down to the island and sample the full range of a truly unusual cuisine.

Left, the pizza of Puerto Rico. **Right**, plain, simple and filling.

If you don't know what you're in for, be warned that Puerto Rico's art scene offers delights to the mind and senses as meaningful and alluring as those of its landscape. This may mean entering a room of carved religious figures (*santos*) in the middle of a bustling city and finding yourself enveloped in their holy silence; or wandering into a museum or gallery in Old San Juan, only to find yourself as taken by a beautifully landscaped 17th-century courtyard as by what you see on the walls; or talking to a local artist or scholar and finding that his passion for the island and its craftsmen is yours.

To be sure, there are frustrations to be encountered. In San Juan the problem centers around a glut of a good thing; finding the best is often a confusing task, with charlatans working next to some of the great artists of the day. Difficulties out on the island are more clearly logistical, with many of Puerto Rico's most fascinating local museums hiding in forgettable outbuildings on the edges of towns. But even the most cursory foray into the island's artistic past and present will be rewarding.

Museum isle: The Institute of Puerto Rican Culture, located in the dazzling Dominican Convent in Old San Juan, owns a vast amount of the island's cultural inheritance, and can guide you to almost anything you fancy. Old San Juan itself is particularly fortunate as an artistic center; besides its nine museums, it boasts a dozen solid contemporary art galleries, a few cooperatives and craft shops of all description. Some of its exhibition spaces are ingenious, perhaps the chief among them being the Arsenal, an army barracks now given over to shows by local artists.

If buying art interests you as much as just looking at it, Old San Juan is certainly the spot to begin your shopping spree. You'll find Pre-Columbian pieces at Galería Los Arcos; and prints as well as paintings at Botello, Coabey, Labiosa and Marrozini. In Santurce, Casa Candina is a charming gallery in a beautiful and quiet hacienda. It's not only the island's center for ceramic arts, but

the site of many important art shows and exhibitions as well. Other galleries await at Plaza Las Américas.

The Museum of the University of Puerto Rico in Río Piedras exhibits only a fifth of its collection, but that small proportion is of absolutely superior quality, from Pre-Columbian art right up to the strongest painters of the present day. But the last word on Puerto Rican art must go to the Ponce Art Museum, envisioned by former Governor Luís Ferré and executed by architect Edward

Durrell Stone. You'll find a more detailed discussion in our Ponce chapter. It will be enough to say here that in a series of dramatically sunlit hexagonal rooms art is reflecting the full range of the drama of human life. From the simplest of faces in Jan van Eyck's "Salvator Mundi" to an overpopulated "Fall of the Rebel Angels" to Rossetti's wonderfully confrontational "Daughters of King Lear," you'll find it impossible not to be moved. Go out of your way to get there and you will not be disappointed.

Art for heart's sake: Many of Puerto Rico's greatest achievements have been in the folk arts, and these retain a broad appeal, whether

Left and **right**, carved religious figures (*santos*) were an early art form.

in the form of *mundillos* (tatted fabrics), *cuatros* (four-stringed guitars) or the festive masks of both Ponce and Loíza. The Ponceño masks are particularly captivating, shaped in forms of animal and devil heads, with hollowed horns, jagged cartoon-style teeth, protruding tongues and furry skin. They originated in medieval Spain, where, during the Lenten season, town rowdies would make the rounds dressed as devils, to terrify sinners into returning to the church for salvation. A habit long since fallen into desuetude in the Old World, it's alive and well in Ponce every February at the Festival of Our Lady of Guadeloupe, Ponce's patron saint.

By contrast, there is an uncanny spiritual particular saints for intercession in healing parts of the body. You can find such *santos* in the Capilla del Cristo in Old San Juan. Though *santos* by the great masters are difficult to come by, there's hardly a home on the island where you won't find at least one *santo* of some sort, greatly revered and passed on from generation to generation.

Locations: The Indian Ceremonial Ballpark at Utuado gives haunting echoes of pre-Columbian life and culture. Here, early Taíno Indians played a more civilized version of the balancing game favored by Mexico's Mayans, in which one had to keep a small ball suspended in the air for long periods of time, hitting it only with shoulders, head and

quiet to be found in Puerto Rican *santos*, arguably the island's greatest contribution to the plastic arts. These wooden religious idols vary greatly in size and shape. The Baroque detail of the earliest pieces reflects both their period origins and the tastes of a Spanish clientele. But as Puerto Rico began to develop a stronger sense of colonial identity, as well as an artisan tradition, *santeros* began to carve figures of a striking simplicity.

The proof of the healing powers of *santos* is said to be attested to by the presence of *milagros* ("miracles"), small silver appendages in shapes of parts of the body. These were donated by people who had prayed to ankles. This version is only "more civilized" on the strength of the fact that the early Taínos were not sacrificed to the gods if they dropped the ball, as their Mexican counterparts were. The dolmen-like stones surrounding the *bateyes*, or playing spaces, show great feeling for the ideal spatial relationship between art and nature.

One finds similar evidence of the vast and various Taíno legacy at the University Museum in Río Piedras, which holds the cultural patrimony of the island. Digs from the last 10 years have been especially abundant in discoveries, some of them dazzling in quality. Amidst the expected artifacts – amulets, potsherds, tools – are some baffling cultural curiosities, like stone collars, great solid yokes at once regal and unbearable. In one intriguing case concerning Puerto Rico's early Arawaks, men bend and sway together in entranced harmony. In another are two partially exposed skeletons, a few broken possessions at their sides.

For all the diversity of her many cultural traditions, it was not until the 18th century that Puerto Rico produced her first major artist in the Western tradition: José Campeche (1752–1809). In spite of never having left the island and having been exposed to European painting only through prints, Campeche still managed to create paintings of mastery.

from behind. In his left hand are the first plans to pave the streets of San Juan; outside in the distance are men laboring busily to make his dream into a reality. It is truly a triumphant picture.

A more accessible painter, and something of a local hero in Puerto Rico, is Francisco Oller (1833–1917). His work is housed in all three main sources: the Institute and the museums at Ponce and Río Piedras. To this day, the extent of his influence on Puerto Rican painting is immeasurable. Unlike Campeche, Oller lived and traveled abroad throughout his life. He studied under Courbet, was an intimate of both Pissarro and Cezanne, painted European royalty, and yet remained

His religious works show a weakness for sentimentality, with their glut of *putti* and pastel clouds, but the inner peace which Campeche succeeds in displaying in his main holy figures dispels all doubt as to his stature as a truly inspired artist. There are two such masterpieces in the Ponce Museum, but it is in a formal portrait which hangs in the Institute of Puerto Rican Culture that one sees Campeche at the height of his powers. The eponymous "Governor Ustauriz" stands in a magnificent room, with sunlight entering

Left, Ponce Art Museum. Above left, Hammock maker's studio; and right, veigante mask artisan.

loyal to – and fiercely proud of – his island homeland. He was a Realist with Impressionist ideas, able to paint gorgeously everything he faced. He was adept at all genres; portraits, still lifes and landscapes like "Hacienda Aurora," which resonates with the colors of Puerto Rico just as much in evidence today.

A piece of work which defies reproduction and is worth a plane ticket to Ponce is Oller's "El Velorio" (The Wake). An enormous painting, it covers an entire wall in the Museum at Río Piedras and illuminates the common man's universe in a fashion not unlike that of Breughel. Here people laugh,

cry, drink, sing and dance about, while on a lace-covered table an almost forgotten, stone-white dead child lies strewn with flowers.

Oller's legacy to Puerto Rican painters has been one not only of technique but of theme as well. Since his time, island painters have taken an overwhelming pride in Puerto Rico's diverse populace and landscape. Miguel Pou and Ramon Frade were among the earliest to follow Oller's lead, doing some spectacular genre work in the early part of this century.

At the Institute, Frade's painting "The Jíbaro" is a splendid homage to Puerto Rico's country farmers. Shyly surveying us with a bunch of plantains in his arms, this tiny old fellow appears to be a giant, with the land miniatured at his feet and his head haloed by a cloud.

The 1940s saw a rise in printmaking which has left that medium one of the most vibrant in Puerto Rico to this day. Funded by the government, printmaking projects lured a slew of fine artists, many of whom are still active. One thinks in particular of Rafael Tufiño, Antonio Martorell, José Rosa and Lorenzo Homar. Posters by Ramon Power show some of the clarity and strength which the best of Puerto Rican artists continue to draw from the medium.

Over the past 30 years, almost all Puerto Rican artists have studied abroad, and the consequence has been a broadening and increasingly avant-garde range of artistic attitudes. Some artists have remained abroad, like Rafael Ferrer, whose work is as popular in New York as it is in San Juan.

Others have returned to work and teach, producing an art with a distinctively Puerto Rican flavor. Myrna Baez falls into this category, her canvases interweaving past and present, inner and outer space. Her "Homage to Vermeer" shows a lone figure in an interior surrealistically touched by landscape. Reflectively, she seems to have loosed a phantom of tropical hubris as she opens the drawer of a nearby table.

The work of Puerto Rico's newer artists is radiant with color and imagination. Among the up-and-coming painters are Juan Ramón Velázquez, Ivette Cabrera and Consuelo Gotay; among the photographers, John Betancourt and Frieda Medín.

Left, the painting *Homage to Vermeer* by the artist Myrna Baez.

Just prior to his death, the world-renowned Argentinian composer, Alberto Ginastera, visited Puerto Rico in order to attend the world premiere of one of his works commissioned by the Pablo Casals Festival. During an interview at the Caribe Hilton, Mr Ginastera's thoughts turned to the song of the *coquí*, the tiny frog that is found only in Puerto Rico and is famous for its persistent and ubiquitous nocturnal calls. "It is the only natural song that I know of," said Mr Ginastera, "which is formed of a perfect own. As a result, there are at least a half-dozen string instruments native to the island, and about which more will be said below. In the absence of many tonal instruments, the settlers made do with percussive ones, which are ready at hand in the various gourds, woods, shoots and beans native to their land. The arrival of West African slaves, who brought with them a well-developed and long history of percussion-based music, accelerated this trend.

Even now, Puerto Ricans are very adept at

seventh." The *coquí* sings a two-note song – "co…kee!" – and these two notes are a perfect seventh apart. It should come, therefore, as no surprise that the island's natural sounds have their unique man-made counterpart. The music of Puerto Rico is *salsa*.

From settlement to salsa: Puerto Ricans have always excelled in music, and the somewhat haphazard course of the island's history has given it a multitude of traditions from which to build a distinctively Puerto Rican sound. The earliest settlers were as enthusiastic about their music as any Spaniards, but deprived of their native string instruments, found themselves in the position of having to create their

making music with whatever happens to be within grabbing distance. No one *owns* a musical performance in Puerto Rico, as one does in other countries. Play a Puerto Rican a piano tune he likes in a bar room or café, and you won't believe your ears when you hear the rhythmic sounds he gets out of a spoon, a wood block, a bead necklace or even his knuckles on the table.

No lack of formality: To be fair, there is a somewhat formalized genre of this very type of music. It's called *plenas* and generally involves a handful of young men creating different rhythms on an amazing variety of hand-held percussion instruments. Some resemble hand-held tympanies, some Irish *bodhrans*, some tambourines, and many of them are homemade. The custom of *plenas* originated among the early blacks of Ponce, but today you can hear its distinctive sounds at any patron saint's festival and occasionally at Plaza Las Armas or Plaza Darsenas in Old San Juan.

This is not to neglect the achievements of this small island in the more traditional forms. It is a haven for the opera, and has its own company; Justino Díaz, the island's finest

before World War I as one of the greatest cellists of his era. After leaving Spain in 1936 as a protest against the Spanish Civil War, he settled in the French Pyrenees, where the first Casals Festival was held in 1950. He visited his mother's homeland in 1956, and spent the final years of his life in Puerto Rico. At the invitation of Governor Luís Muñoz Marín, he founded a Puerto Rican Casals Festival in 1957, which must rank as the greatest cultural event in the Antilles, and a formidable one by world standards. In later

male vocalist, has impressed critics from New York to Milan. The Puerto Rico Symphony Orchestra, despite being relatively young, is probably the best in the Caribbean, and has premiered works by some of Latin America's finest composers, many of them at the Casals Festivals.

It is Pablo Casals who, more than any other Puerto Rican resident, is responsible for the upsurge of interest and proficiency in classical performance in Puerto Rico in recent years. Born in Catalonia in 1876 of a Puerto Rican mother, Casals was recognized almost

years, Casals went on to form the Puerto Rican Symphony Orchestra and the Puerto Rican Conservatory of Music. On his death at the age of 97 in 1973, he considered himself a Puerto Rican; his countrymen considered him one of their national heroes.

Rhythm of the tropics: Salsa is what happens when Afro-Caribbean music meets big-band jazz. Its roots may be found in the early explorations of Puerto Rican Tito Puente and Cuban musicians in New York City clubs following World War II. After serving three years in the United States Navy, Puente studied percussion at the Julliard School on New York's West Side. He was soon playing

Left, Friday night disco. **Above**, fiesta band.

and composing for top bandleaders like Machito and Pupi Campo, and he quickly proceeded to establish his own orchestra. Puente's Latin Jazz Ensemble continues to delight audiences throughout the world.

In an interview in *Latin US* magazine, Puente was asked to define salsa: "As you know, salsa in Spanish means "sauce," and we use it mostly as a condiment for our foods... salsa in general is all our fast Latin music put together: the merengue, the rumba, the mambo, the cha-cha, the guaguanco, boogaloo, all of it is salsa... in Latin music, we have many different types of rhythms, such as ballads (boleros), rancheros, tangos, and, of course, salsa."

Luz, which despite its name is Japanese.

Puerto Rican music has evolved into the salsa beat; music has played a crucial role in Puerto Rican society and culture for as long as there have been Puerto Ricans. During Spanish rule, the *danza* was the chief form of entertainment for the *criollo* aristocracy; it reached its high point in the late 19th century when Morel Campos and other masters gave it a popularity that redounded back to Spain. This highly stylized tradition of music and its accompanying dance movements are preserved by several local ensembles in Puerto Rico. The *danza* is characterized by a string orchestra, woodwinds, and a formal ambience. *La Borinqueña*, the Puerto Rican na-

The salsa band is usually composed of a lead vocalist and chorus, a piano, a bass, a horn section and a heavy assortment of percussion instruments (bongos, conga, maracas, güiros, timbales, claves, and the ever-present cowbell). The overall effect is mesmerizing, the rhythm contagious.

Traditional music for the world: Salsa has placed Puerto Rico on the map of popular music. Says Puente: "It's totally unexpected to see Belgians, Swedes, Finns and Danes swing to the Latin Beat... The bands there are playing more salsa than we are." Indeed, one of the most popular international salsa bands isn't even Puerto Rican – it's Orchestra de la

tional anthem, is a *danza*.

A more popular and widely practised Puerto Rican musical tradition is the *aquinaldo*, a song performed around the Christmas and Three Kings holiday, usually in the form of an *asalto*. The *asalto* is a charming tradition which dates back to the 19th century, and perhaps earlier. It goes along with the unrestrained partying of the holiday season. It is customary at an *asalto* to feast on *lechón asao* (roast suckling pig), *yucca* (a local potato-like root), *arroz con*

Above, traditional music-makers in the mountain town of San Sebastián.

pollo (chicken with rice), *gandules* (local peas) and *palos de ron* (well, okay, so they have some rum). Following the feast, a group of celebrants stumbles from house to house, waking the residents and singing *aquinaldos*. The members of each household are expected to join the *asalto* as it moves throughout the neighborhood. Recordings of these genial songs are available as performed by a *trulla*, which is any professional group of *aquinaldo* singers.

The *décima* is arguably the most appealing form of traditional Puerto Rican music. It is the vehicle through which the *jíbaro* expresses his joys and frustrations; it is the poetry of the Puerto Rican soul. Instrumentation for the *décima* consists of a number of three-, four- and six-stringed instruments (called appropriately the *tres, cuatro* and *seis*); a minimal rhythm is kept up by claves or the *güiro*.

The trademark of the *décima* is verbal improvisation. Often, two singers will alternate stanzas, trying to outboast each other with rhyming tales of luscious fruit, pretty women or physical prowess. The verbal jousting is fueled by the audience. The similarity between the *décima* and the verbal duelling of rap DJs is striking.

In contemporary Puerto Rico, salsa is king, but who is the King of Salsa? The classics include Willie Colón, Panamanian singer-turned-politician Rubén Blades, recently deceased Hector Lavoe, El Gran Combo de Puerto Rico and the Fania All-Stars.

Puerto Rico's biggest salsa star is Gilberto Santa Rosa (a protégé of Willie Rosario), affectionately known as "Gilbertito."

In addition to salsa, merengue groups from the nearby Dominican Republic have become very popular. In fact, it is the preferred dance music at many Puerto Rican parties. Some locals, led by Olga Tañon, have been able to cash in on the fast-paced merengue sound with albums and concert appearances.

The pre-pubescent vote favors Menudo: young *puertorriqueños* have probably stained more fanmag photos of Menudo with tears than men have stained tissues during the queen of salsa Isabel Chacón's show. But that's a book in itself. Whatever the individual's taste, salsa continues as one of the hottest forms of popular music in the world.

Willie Colón and his band have produced some of the most inspired salsa to date. The album "Siembra," a collaboration with Rubén Blades, is easily one of the hottest discs around. The songs on "Siembra" show the rhythmic complexity which is at the core of salsa, as well as the thematic motifs which tie all of salsa together. "Pedro Navaja" tells the story of a street tough and his inevitable demise. Blades croons the final verse, describing the scene after a gunfight:

*And believe me people, although there
was noise, nobody came out. There were
no busybodies, no questions asked, and
nobody cried. Only a drunk bumped into
the two bodies, and picked up the revolver, the knife and the dollars and
marched off; and stumbling, he went on
his way singing off-tune the chorus that
I bring you that gives the message of my
song. Life gives you surprises, surprises
will give you life, Oh, God!*

He who lives by violence dies by violence; Colón and Blades are not the first salsa singers to choose this theme for a musical starting point.

Colón's talent sparkles in other collaborative efforts. His 1977 recording with Celia Cruz, entitled "Only They Could Have Made This Album," is a superb example of salsa's African roots. The songs from "Pun Pun Catalu," "Rinkinkalla," and "Burundanga" make use of African linguistic and musical references. "Burundanga" is an outgrowth of the music of *santería*, the Afro-Caribbean religious cult.

Of the bands, El Gran Combo (de Puerto Rico) has had great success since the early 1960s, probably owing to their songs' optimism and enthusiasm. They have great musical talent, a good sense of humor, and a massive popular following.

The road to a better future (like Puerto Rican Spanish) is not always easy to follow, and the song "Resignación" suggest an amusing relief for the "estress" of making a fulfilling life for one's self.

*Tell me Mr. Psychiatrist, what should I
   do?
I've lost my friends and my woman, too.
I'm going to prescribe "bothers me
   not" potion,
Along with an ointment and salve of
   "and so what."
And if you know English and things
   continue ugly
Take five pills of "I don't care."*

PLACES

Puerto Rico? That's beaches, right, and *paradors* (hotels in characterful ancient buildings) and old Spanish forts tossed in with a few frosty rum drinks? Well, yes and no. You won't want to miss Old San Juan's colorful streets, or standing on El Morro's walls, looking out into the Atlantic at the ghosts of 16th-century British invaders, and you certainly shouldn't leave the island without tasting a *piña colada* – but there are far more places to see and understand than those fringed with surf and sand.

We've started this section of the book in Puerto Rico's most populous area, San Juan. Old San Juan, an eight-block area on a small peninsula, harkens back to the 16th-century, but scant miles away in Hato Rey and Río Piedras, modern commerce is being conducted in sleek steel and glass corporate offices.

If metropolitan San Juan is the most humanly populated area of the island, then the Northeast is the most geographically populated. The range of terrain in the region, from beaches to dense rain forest to secluded islands is staggering. The Northeast's natural attractions draw the crowds.

Head out to the Northwest coast and you'll be able to travel around the oddly-scaled karst mountain region. Limestone formations rise above the island's most historic cities – Arecibo, Lares, San Sebastián and Isabela.

Those karstic mountains rise up into the island's spine – the Cordillera Central. Here, the Ruta Panoramica will take the adventurous driver from one end of the range to the other, affording spectacular views all the while.

And if you cross over the mountains to the South and Southwest regions of the island, you'll realize fully the relaxed pace of life on the island. There's Ponce, a pearl of a city, on the coast, but if you're tired of the urban hustle, you'll never be at a loss to find a quiet place to sit in the sun.

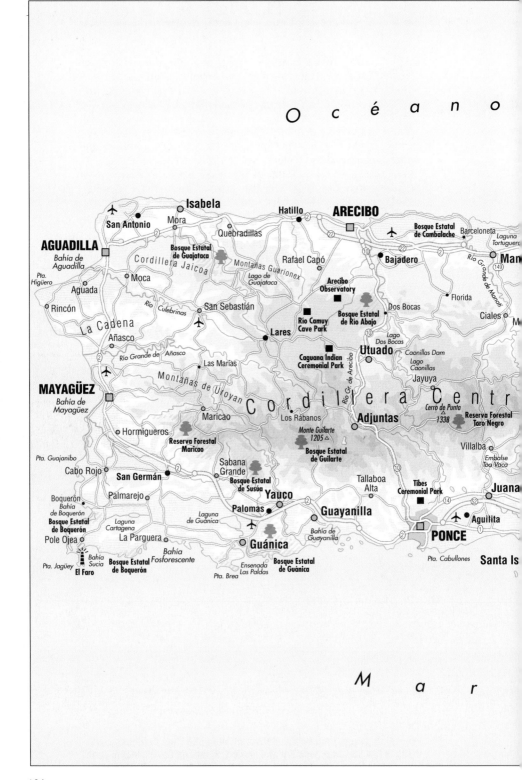

O c é a n o

Isabela
Hatillo
ARECIBO
✈ San Antonio
Mora
Quebradillas
Bosque Estatal
de Cambalache
Barceloneta
Laguna
Tortuguero
AGUADILLA
Bahía de
Aguadilla
Bosque Estatal
de Guajataca
Rafael Capó
22
Bajadero
Río Grande de Manatí
Man
149
Cordillera Jaicoa
Montañas Guarionex
10
Pta.
Higüero
Moca
Lago de
Guajataca
Arecibo
Observatory
Aguada
Florida
Rincón
Río Culebrinas
San Sebastián
Río Camuy
Cave Park
Bosque Estatal
de Río Abajo
Dos Bocas
Ciales
M
La Cadena
Lares
Lago
Dos Bocas
Añasco
Río Grande de Añasco
Las Marías
Caguana Indian
Ceremonial Park
Utuado
Caonillas Dam
Lago
Caonillas
Jayuya
MAYAGÜEZ
Montañas de Uroyan
Cordillera Centr
Bahía de
Mayagüez
Maricao
Los Rábanos
Río Gr. de Arecibo
Adjuntas
Cerro de Punta
1338
Reserva Forestal
Toro Negro
Hormigueros
Reserva Forestal
Maricao
Monte Guilarte
1205
Villalba
Pta. Guajanibo
Sabana
Grande
Bosque Estatal
de Guilarte
Embalse
Toa Vaca
Cabo Rojo
Bosque Estatal
de Susúa
Tallaboa
Alta
Tibes
Ceremonial Park
10
San Germán
Yauco
Juana
Boquerón
Bahía
de Boquerón
Palmarejo
Laguna
de Guánica
Palomas
Guayanilla
14
52
Bosque Estatal
de Boquerón
Laguna
Cartagena
Aguilita
Pole Ojea
La Parguera
Bahía
Fosforescente
Bahía de
Guayanilla
PONCE
Bahía
Sucia
Bosque Estatal
de Boquerón
Guánica
Pta. Cabullones
Santa Is
Pta. Jagüey
El Faro
Ensenada
Las Paldas
Bosque Estatal
de Guánica
Pta. Brea

M a r

104

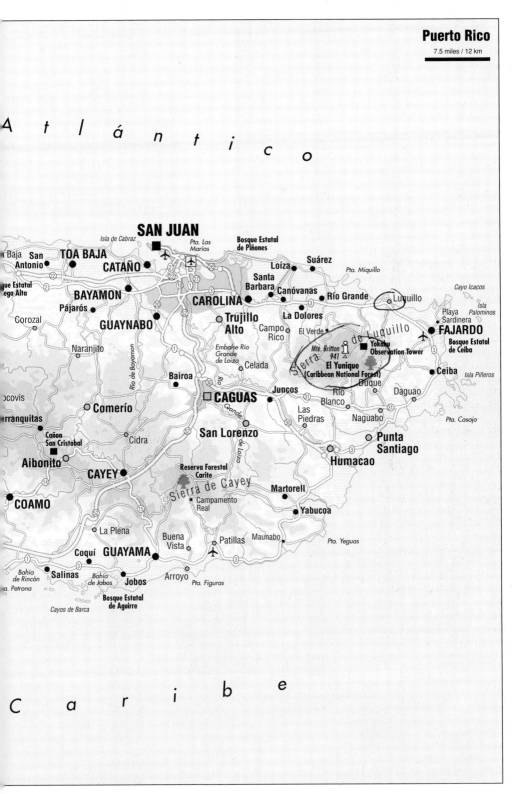

A t l á n t i c o

SAN JUAN

Isla de Cabraz *Pta. Las Marías* Bosque Estatal de Piñones

TOA BAJA CATAÑO Loíza Suárez *Pta. Miquillo*

Baja San Antonio Santa Barbara Canóvanas *Cayo Icacos*

ue Estatal ega Alta BAYAMON CAROLINA Río Grande Luquillo *Isla Palominos*

Pájarós Playa Sardinera

Corozal GUAYNABO Trujillo Alto La Dolores El Verde FAJARDO

Naranjito Campo Rico *Embalse Río Grande de Loíza* Sierra de Luquillo Yokahu Observation Tower Bosque Estatal de Ceiba

Río de Bayamon Celada *Mte. Britton 941* El Yunique (Caribbean National Forest) Ceiba *Isla Piñeros*

Bairoa Duque

ocovis Juncos Río Blanco Daguao

rranquitas CAGUAS Las Piedras Naguabo *Pta. Casajo*

Comerío Grande San Lorenzo Humacao Punta Santiago

Cañon San Cristobal Cidra de Loíza

Aibonito Reserva Forestal Carite Martorell

COAMO CAYEY Sierra de Cayey Campamento Real Yabucoa

La Plena Buena Vista Patillas Maunabo *Pta. Yeguas*

Coquí GUAYAMA

Bahía de Rincón Salinas *Bahía de Jobos* Jobos Arroyo *Pta. Figuras*

a. Petrona Bosque Estatal de Aguirre

Cayos de Barca

C a r i b e

105

SAN JUAN

Imagine a city that looks like Paris painted pink, orange, pastel green, and white; a city paved in iron, with streets the color of thunderclouds; a banking center for a dozen island nations; an intellectual hotspot, with a handful of top-notch universities and a vibrant art scene; a tropical city, which has never had frost.

San Juan is hard to envision until one has seen it, and hard to describe even when one has seen it. Aside from descriptions of stunning scenic beauty, or avowals of a magnificent historical legacy, it is difficult to capture what is so captivating in the city. Perhaps it is the ambiguity of being one of the oldest of Spanish cities in the New World and being subject to the government of an English-speaking power, having "two citizenships, two flags, two national anthems."

But, if so, what is it that makes San Juan so special among Puerto Rican cities? Certainly not its size alone. Perhaps again it is the diversity of this metropolitan area of 1.6 million people which attracts. How can a modern city encompass the quaintness of Old San Juan and the brashness of the Hato Rey business district, the timeless seaside life of Boca de Cangrejos and the modernity of Bayamón, the glitter of the Condado and the austerity of La Perla?

It probably can't. San Juan is all you have heard it would be. And more. And less. For no one can possibly have the breadth of interest to enjoy all its charms. This makes San Juan a city to captivate any taste. Beauty is in the eye of the creator here; you choose your own San Juan.

Preceding pages: strolling along one of Old San Juan's many-hued streets. **Left**, colonial style in Old San Juan.

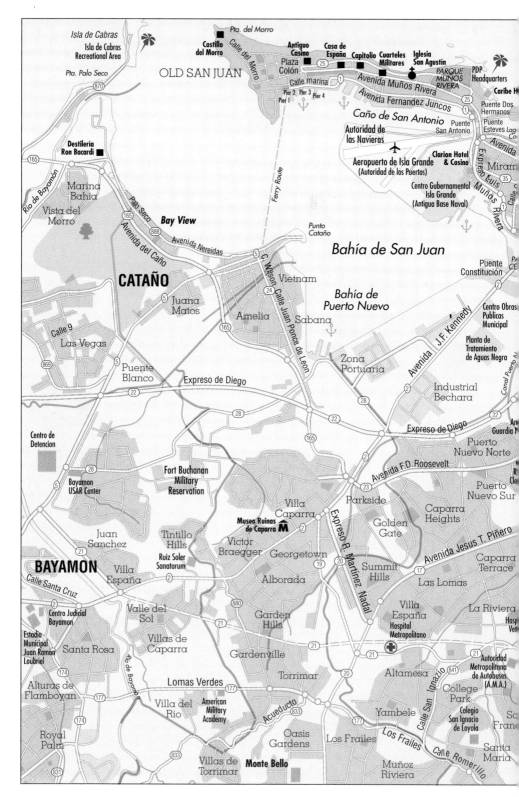

Isla de Cabras
Isla de Cabras
Recreational Area
Pta. Palo Seco
870

Destileria
Ron Bacardi
165

Marina
Bahía
Vista del
Morro
Rio de Bayamón

Palo Seco
165
Avenida del Caño
888

Bay View
Avenida Nereidas

CATAÑO
Juana
Matos
5
165

Calle 9
Las Vegas
869

Puente
Blanco
5
22

Centro de
Detencion
28
5
Bayamon
USAR Center

Juan
Sanchez
21

BAYAMON
Calle Santa Cruz
Villa
España
2

Centro Judicial
Bayamon
2

Estadio
Municipal
Juan Ramon
Loubriel
174

Santa Rosa

Alturas de
Flamboyan
174
177

Royal
Palm
831

Pta. del Morro
Castillo
del Morro
Calle del Morro

OLD SAN JUAN
Pier 2 Pier 3 Pier 4
Pier 1
Calle marina

Antiguo
Casino
Plaza
Colón
25

Casa de
España
Capitolio
Cuarteles
Militares
Iglesia
San Agustin
Avenida Muños Rivera
1
Avenida Fernandez Juncos

Caño de San Antonio
Puente
San Antonio
Autoridad de
las Navieras

Aeropuerto de Isla Grande
(Autoridad de los Puertos)

Clarion Hotel
& Casino

Centro Gubernamental
Isla Grande
(Antigua Base Naval)

PARQUE
MUÑOS
RIVERA
PDP
Headquarters
Caribe H

25
1
Puente Dos
Hermanos
Puente
Esteves Lag
Avenida
Expreso Luis
Muñoz Rivera
35
Miram

Punto
Cataño

Bahía de San Juan
Puente
Constitución
CE
2

C. Wilson
Vietnam
5
24
Amelia
Sabana

Bahía de
Puerto Nuevo
Zona
Portuaria

Centro Obras
Publicas
Municipal

Planta de
Tratamiento
de Aguas Negra

Calle Juan Ponce de Leon

Expreso de Diego
28
22
165

Avenida J.F. Kennedy
2
Industrial
Bechara
28
Expreso de Diego
22
An
Guardia N

Puerto
Nuevo Norte

2
Avenida F.D. Roosevelt
23
Puerto
Nuevo Sur

Fort Buchanan
Military
Reservation

Villa
Caparra
Parkside
Caparra
Heights

Golden
Gate

Museo Ruinas
de Caparra M
2

Tintillo
Hills
Ruiz Soler
Sanatorum

Victor
Braegger
Georgetown
19

Summit
Hills
Las Lomas
17
Caparra
Terrace

Valle del
Sol
880

Alborada
20

Villa
España
Hospital
Metropolitano
La Riviera
Hosp
Vet

Villas de
Caparra
21

Garden
Hills
21

Gardenville
21

Expreso R. Martinez Nadal

Altamesa
21
Autoridad
Metropolitana
de Autobuses
(A.M.A.)
841

Lomas Verdes
177
Torrimar
20

Villa del
Rio
American
Military
Academy
Acueducto
833

Oasis
Gardens
Los Frailes

Yambele
Colegio
San Ignacio
de Loyola

College
Park
So
Fran

Calle San Ignacio
Santa
Maria

Villas de
Torrimar
Monte Bello
833

Muñoz
Riviera
Los Frailes
Calle Romerillo
Santa

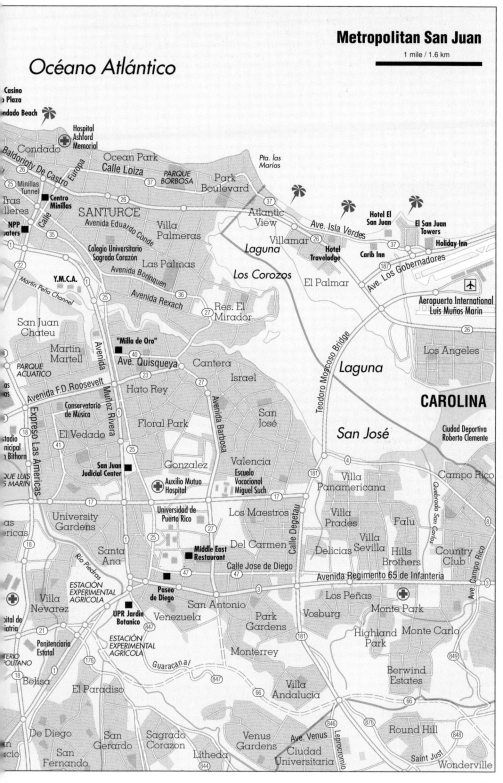

Océano Atlántico

Casino
Plaza
Condado Beach

Condado

Baldorioty De Castro

Hospital
Ashford
Memorial

Ocean Park
Calle Loiza

PARQUE
BORBOSA

Park
Boulevard

Pta. las
Marias

26
25 Minillas
Tunnel

Tras
lleres

Centro
Minillas

SANTURCE

Avenida Eduardo Conde

Villa
Palmeras

Atlantic
View

Villamar

Ave. Isla Verdes

Hotel El
San Juan

El San Juan
Towers

Holiday Inn

NPP
uaters

35

Colegio Universitario
Sagrada Corazón

Las Palmas

Laguna

Los Corozos

Villamar

26

Hotel
Travelodge

Carib Inn

El Palmar

187

Ave. Los Gobernadores

22

Y.M.C.A.

Avenida Borinquen

Martin Peña Channel

25

Avenida Rexach

36

Res. El
Mirador

27

Aeropuerto International
Luis Muños Marin

26

San Juan
Chateu

Martin
Martell

PARQUE
ACUATICO

"Milla de Oro"

40

Ave. Quisqueya

23

Cantera

Israel

Laguna

Los Angeles

Teodoro Moscoso Bridge

Avenida

Muñoz Rivera

Hato Rey

San
José

San José

CAROLINA

Avenida F.D. Roosevelt

Conservatorio
de Música

Floral Park

Avenida Barbosa

Ciudad Deportiva
Roberto Clemente

QUE LUIS
S MARIN

El Vedado

41

Expreso Las Americas

San Juan
Judicial Center

Gonzalez

Valencia

Escuela
Vocacional
Miguel Such

17

4

Villa
Panamericana

Villa
Prades

Campo Rico

8

25

Auxilio Mutuo
Hospital

181

Falu

Universidad de
Puerto Rico

Los Maestros

Calle Degetau

Villa
Sevilla

University
Gardens

17

18

Santa
Ana

25

Del Carmen

27

Delicias

Hills
Brothers

Country
Club

Rio Piedras

Middle East
Restaurant

47

Calle Jose de Diego

Avenida Regimento 65 de Infanteria

3

Quebrada San Carlos

Ave. Campo Rico

ESTACIÓN
EXPERIMENTAL
AGRICOLA

47

Paseo
de Diego

San Antonio

Vosburg

Los Peñas

Monte Park

Villa
Nevarez

21

UPR Jardin
Botanico

847

Venezuela

Park
Gardens

181

Monte Carlo

Highland
Park

ital de
iatria

Penitenciaria
Estatal

ESTACIÓN
EXPERIMENTAL
AGRICOLA

176

Monterrey

849

ERIO
OLITANO

18

Belisa

1

El Paradiso

Guaracanal

847

Villa
Andalucia

66

Berwind
Estates

66

De Diego

San
Gerardo

Sagrado
Corazon

Venus
Gardens

Ave. Venus

846

876

Round Hill

848

San
Fernando

Litheda

844

Ciudad
Universitaria

Leprocromio

Saint Just

Wonderville

OLD SAN JUAN

No matter how much history is crammed into the seven narrow city blocks of Old San Juan, no matter how seductive the pastel-and-wrought-iron Spanish colonial houses may seem, no matter how chock-to-the-brim with opportunities for socializing and partying this city may be, it is something altogether more spiritual that attracts Puerto Ricans and foreigners alike to San Juan.

There is something in the place that traps travelers and forces them to lead their vacations at the pace at which a vacation should properly be led. If you've rushed through Old San Juan, you certainly have not been there. Get a good pair of walking shoes and ramble; a car is as much a liability as it is an asset here, anyway.

This oldest of American cities has iron streets, filled in with *adoquines*, or blocks of slag, from the lowland smelting mills of Spain's 16th-century empire. It has two of the most invulnerable forts ever constructed, which are connected by walls that circle a peninsula. It has some of the finest restaurants and bars in the Caribbean. And the city is full of art galleries.

It is also full of some of the loudest tourists you'll meet anywhere. If you are one of them, best wishes. If not, it might be mentioned that even within its tiny area, Old San Juan has an endless supply of undiscovered attractions. These are what lead second-time visitors to call for a taxi to Old San Juan as soon as they step off the plane at Luis Muñoz Marín International Airport.

Into the city: As Puerto Rico's Spanish history begins with Columbus, Old San Juan begins in the **Plaza Colón**, or Columbus Square, a quadrangle built around a commemorative statue of the explorer. It is here that the high-speed, heavily trafficked Avenidas Ponce de León and Muñoz Rivera give way to the narrow and scarcely navigable grid that is Old San Juan. If you're without a car this will be your last stop on the municipal bus or *publico*. If you are driving, you should now start looking for a place to park.

Located at the southeastern corner of the Old San Juan quadrant, Plaza Colón is an ideal spot for fanning out on a walking tour of the city. The square itself offers a good introductory stroll. On its south side is the **Teatro Tapia y Rivera**, a tasteful, ochre hacienda-like structure dating from 1826 and beautifully restored in the mid-1970s.

For all its other cultural achievements, Puerto Rico has produced very little theater of note; Alejandro Tapia y Rivera (1826–82), after whom the theater is named, is the earliest and perhaps most notable exception. Today the theater premieres plays by Latin America's most exciting contemporary dramatists. Across the street from the theater on the plaza's eastern side is the **Old Casino of Puerto Rico**, built shortly after the American capture of Puerto Rico but harking back architecturally to the Spanish reign.

Ironically, if somewhat predictably, the path most tourists take into Old San

Left, Friday night *paseo*. **Right**, objet d'art in one of San Juan's galleries.

Juan is the least characteristic of the city. **Calle Fortaleza** is, at least for three blocks, as cluttered with bargain basements, souvenir shops and second rate hotels as any place in the city. Fortunately, Calle Fortaleza is just as crowded with architectural wonders. The first right along the street is **Callejón de la Capilla**, a romantic, lantern-lit alleyway which passes a decent *colmado* and an unpretentious outdoor café as it arcs uphill to Calle San Francisco.

At the corner of Fortaleza and Callejón de la Capilla, the **Casa del Callejón**, an 18th-century residence, houses two charming museums.

The **Museum of Colonial Architecture**, on the first floor, has an impressive collection of blueprints, city plans and photographs, but is certainly more satisfying to those who are already familiar with the layout of San Juan. Upstairs, the **Museum of the Puerto Rican Family** has on display a carefully reconstructed Puerto Rican home of a century ago.

Continuing on Calle Fortaleza, turn right on Calle Tanca for a bit of relaxation in the sloping Plaza Salvador Brau, or left down Calle Tanca towards the piers of San Juan Port. Every weekend night, Calle Tanca is filled with throngs of San Juan's teenagers queuing up for admission to its discos and bars.

Most ports which serve a large number of cruise ships end up looking rather like jungles of cranes and heavy machinery. San Juan, which takes more cruise traffic than any port in the Caribbean, is an exception. The port not only benefits from the tastefulness of its more utilitarian maritime buildings (the pink, mock-colonial United States Customs House is a good example), but actually boasts a beautiful cityscape as well.

The waterfront promises to become even more beautiful in 1997, when the ambitious $120 million **Frente Portuario** complex is finished. The first of a three-phase project designed to transform the once-seedy area, this Mediterranean-style megaproject will have 200 condominium apartments in three buildings, a 242-room Wyndham Hotel

The view from just offshore.

and Casino, two office towers, a 603-space parking garage and 110,000 square feet of retail space will be available upon completion.

Frente Portuario, designed to ensure that it blends in with the rest of Old San Juan, will feature cobblestone-like paved boulevards lined with wrought-iron lamps and red-tiled roofs. Visitors will browse through art galleries, eateries and boutiques.

The government has already spent $100 million to renovate half a dozen cruise-ship ports along the waterfront. Some of the world's largest cruise ships, including Royal Caribbean Lines' *Monarch of the Seas* and its twin sister, *Sovereign of the Seas*, regularly call here. From Pier 2, you can also take the ferry to Cataño, home of the Bacardí rum distillery. At 50 cents a passenger, this ferry is truly one of Puerto Rico's great bargains.

Plaza de Hostos is an oasis of shade in a square full of *adoquines* (iron bricks). Named after the 19th-century *independentista* scholar, it provides a haven for sunburnt tourists and locals alike; the square must be the domino capital of the Caribbean. Looming over the plaza is the original office of the **Banco Popular de Puerto Rico**, which is surely one of the great modern architectural triumphs of the Caribbean. This brawny, 10-story mass, built in the mid-1930s, is unashamedly art deco. Heavy cameo eagles brood over the main entrance, which is lettered in sans-serif gilt intaglio. Elongated windows with prominent pastel mullions run the full height of a faintly apsidal facade.

The pier area is particularly fortunate in its culinary offerings. **Calle Tetuán** has a number of first-rate restaurants from the Yukiyu (Japanese) to La Chaumière (French) but is marred somewhat by the massive parking garage it shares with Calle Recinto Sur.

Whether approaching uphill on Calle Cruz from Plaza de Hostos, or via Calle Fortaleza from Plaza Colón, almost all travelers pass through the workaday heart of Old San Juan, centering around the **City Hall** (*Alcaldía*) and the adja-

1 La Casita
2 El Arsenal
3 La Princesa
4 Puerta de San Juan
5 La Fortaleza
6 Museo Felisa Rincón de Gautier
7 Plazuela de la Rogativa
8 Casa Blanca
9 Catedral de San Juan
10 Capilla del Cristo
11 Casa del Libro
12 Centro Nacional de Artes Populares y Artesanías
13 Plaza de Armas
14 Alcaldía (City Hall)
15 Plaza de Colón
16 El Castillo de San Cristóbal
17 Museo de Arte e Historia de San Juan
18 Museo de Pablo Casals
19 Casa de las Contrafuertes
20 Plaza de San José
21 Iglesia de San José
22 Convento Dominican
23 Escuela de Artes Plásticas
24 El Castillo del Morro

Old San Juan
0.25 miles / 400 m

cent Plaza de Armas. City Hall was begun in 1602 to be a replica of Madrid's. What works in Europe seems rather somber for the Antilles, but it is an attractive building nonetheless, one whose charms are enhanced by the fact that small businesses operate within the same arch-covered block as the local government. The plaza is no less historic, having served, in the days before soldiers were permanently billeted in San Juan, as the training field for Spanish soldiers sent out from Europe in order to defend the island.

Nonetheless, the main streets along the **Plaza de Armas** have the unpretentious likeability of a business district, rather than the imposing sense of history of much of San Juan. **Calle San Francisco** is a friendly mix of tourist shops and government buildings, while the part of Calle Fortaleza just south of the plaza is an engaging few blocks of restaurants and department stores.

Worth a visit is **The Butterfly People**, an atmospheric restaurant, overlooking a placid courtyard. It's all very peaceful and aesthetic; walls are covered with thousands and thousands of examples of native butterflies.

Across the street, **González Padín** is the granddaddy of Puerto Rico's department stores. When it was built at the turn of the century, it was the tallest structure on the island. Down Calle San José is **The Book Store**, with the largest selection of English titles in Old San Juan, as well as a number of North American periodicals.

After examining the mosaic work on the facade of the apartment opposite and perhaps watching the cruise boats arrive and depart in San Juan bay directly below, buy a copy of the *New York Times* and take it into the **Cafeteria Los Amigos** next door. Natives consider the coffee here – thick, dark, and served in tiny paper cups – the best bargain in Old San Juan. Rules of conduct for Los Amigos are posted prominently behind the counter, among them *No discuta politica aqui* (Don't discuss politics here).

La Fortaleza: Calle Fortaleza grows

Callejón de la Capilla.

more and more dignified as it approaches **La Fortaleza** itself. This chalk-white wonder of a fortress is the oldest continuously inhabited executive mansion in the New World. Construction began in 1532 and was completed in 1540, and it serves to this day as the residence of the Governor of Puerto Rico. It is an architectural wonder but strategically it was always inadequate. This was apparent even to the Spanish architects, who decided that the nubby peninsula on which La Fortaleza was being built did not command enough of San Juan Bay to protect completely against invasion from the sea. Accordingly, construction of the massive fort at the tip of the San Juan Peninsula – El Morro – began in the 1540s.

The 1588 sinking of the Spanish Armada made the West Indian possessions of the Spanish Crown more vulnerable than ever, with the result that even more Puerto Rican colonists clamored for greater fortification. By 1595, Queen Elizabeth, hearing of 2 million ducats of gold stored in La Fortaleza, quickly dispatched Sir Francis Drake, whose ambitions included not only the great bounty of gold, but all the Spanish lands of the New World as well. Drake arrived in San Juan in late November of that year. He stopped across the bay at Isla de Cabras, and launched a flotilla of several dozen ships. Ten would never go back to England, and 400 English sailors would rest forever beneath San Juan harbor. Drake's own cabin was torn apart by a mortar shell during the invasion.

Perhaps the Spanish grew complacent after the first thwarted invasion of their colonial capital, for in June 1598, the Duke of Cumberland was able to land a force of about 1,000 men in the area of Puerta de Tierra, and march on to San Juan.

British invasion: The 400 Spanish soldiers defending the city were suffering from a severe epidemic but put up a valiant resistance, enduring a 15-day siege inside El Morro before capitulating. The Union Jack flew over the walls of La Fortaleza. The British were

La Fortaleza.

hounded by Spanish colonists almost immediately but it was less Spanish resistance than British *lack* of resistance to the same epidemic that led them to give in. In a matter of several weeks after the invasion, Cumberland sailed for home, having lost over 400 sailors, to leave San Juan to recover in peace for another 27 years.

The year 1625 saw the final occupation of La Fortaleza during colonial times. A Dutch fleet under the command of Boudewijn Hendrikszoon swiftly moved into San Juan Bay and set up a beachhead between El Morro and La Fortaleza.

The Dutch burned much of the city to the ground, including much of La Fortaleza. Reconstruction of La Fortaleza began in 1640; the building was expanded in 1800 and 1846. Guided tours of the building are trips through periods of La Fortaleza's architectural and military history.

Calle del Cristo (Christ's Street) is the most alluring of Old San Juan's thoroughfares, an intoxicating avenue of sights and sounds, of romance and history. Running from a point high above San Juan Bay, Calle del Cristo arches to an even higher perch above San Juan's Atlantic shore, where El Morro looks sternly out to sea. It can claim Old San Juan's most popular park, its most underrated museum, most famous cathedral and its finest bar.

This adventure in *adoquines* begins at the **Parque de las Palomas** (Pigeon Park), a part of the city walls which thousands of pigeons have made their home. Fabulous views of the bay make Parque de las Palomas a popular spot for lovers and an even more popular spot for aspiring ones.

Building with love: Love almost certainly played a decisive part in the construction of the quaint **Capilla del Cristo** (Chapel of Christ). Romantic legend has it that, during an 18th-century horse race, one of two competing riders failed to make a left turn onto Calle Tetuán and plummeted over the massive cliffs, seemingly to his death. When he survived, astounded locals constructed a

Pigeons and friends in Palomas Park.

chapel to commemorate Christ's intercession. Others claim that the race was really a duel over a comely young woman between two chivalrous *enamorados*. One fell to his death and the chapel was built both to commemorate the tragedy and to block off Calle del Cristo to prevent such a mishap from ever occurring again.

The peninsula stretching below the Cristo Chapel is known as **La Puntilla**. Today it houses a few official buildings and a somewhat swank modern condominium complex.

A short walk up Calle del Cristo on the right is one of Puerto Rico's most enchanting and least-known museums. The **Casa del Libro** is a breezy, parqueted sanctuary which is chock-full of fine European illuminated manuscripts as well as work by local artists and illustrators and an excellent selection of postcards.

Next door, the **Centro Nacional de Artes Populares y Artesanías** (Popular Arts and Crafts Center) houses a collection of paintings from the 18th century to the present; a variety of island crafts are also displayed and offered for sale.

Half a dozen eateries crowd this end of Calle del Cristo, though none are as good as **Café Callaloo**, a Caribbean-style restaurant run by a Trinidadian chef married to a local newspaper editor. This outdoor cafe's homemade chicken curry, served with green salad, fresh vegetables, rice, beans and plantains, is arguably the best to be found in Puerto Rico.

Any aesthetic overdose one suffers on the south part of Calle del Cristo can be cured with a bracing *piña colada* in one of the bars on the north side. A plaque around the corner on Calle Fortaleza claims that a bar which once occupied the site of what is now a jewelry store was the birthplace of the *piña colada* in 1963. This is nonsense, of course, but the *piña colada* is at home anywhere in the city.

A cathedral and a convent: Ascending Cristo Street, even the most skeptical of travelers will begin to see what he came

to San Juan for. On the right, usually bathed in sunlight at afternoon, is the **San Juan Cathedral**, a fabulous beige-and-white structure that must count among the most important houses of worship in the west. It was here that Sebastián Ramírez, the first bishop to be consecrated in the New World, was ordained.

The beauty of the church's exterior is immediately perceptible. Its three tiers of white pilaster and arch mount to a simple cross at the church's pinnacle. The three brick-red and white cupolas atop the church are among San Juan's most photogenic objects, and must themselves lure many visitors to the island each year.

But the interior of the church is not as easy to appreciate for anyone who thinks of cathedrals primarily in their French, German, or English incarnations. For one, the floor is of a black parquet, which seems to belie the solemnity of the building. The brown and ochre *trompe l'oeil* ceiling is pretty, but it appears too close to the worshipper's eye. The Cathedral really needs several visits but will in time reward the most discerning.

Among the highlights of the Cathedral are **Ponce de León's gravestone**, with an understated virgin warrior glancing down at the body and the red script of the epitaph, and the glittering blue statue of **La Virgen de Providencia**, Puerto Rico's patroness, located nearby. Pius' remains are to be found in a glass case containing a macabre plaster figure of the saint, to the rear of the altar. There's another such effigy, of a prostrate Jesus, in the **Chapel of Souls in Purgatory** which is in the Cathedral's right nave.

Directly across Calle del Cristo from the Cathedral is **El Gran Convento**, now a luxury hotel, established in 1651 as a convent for Carmelite nuns, San Juan's first. When the nuns moved to Santurce in the early part of this century, the convent fell into disrepair. It was restored only after World War II, in a major project that took several years. **Juice for sale.**

originals, all the interior decor fits in harmoniously with the conception of a nunnery-turned-hotel.

El Batey, across Calle del Cristo from the Convento, is a bar wrapped up in the cultural and intellectual life of its city in a way that few bars ever manage to achieve. Not many travelers pass through the city without making at least one visit to this old-world wonder, whose regular clientele is an even mix of American and European expatriates and young locals. *Batey* is a Taíno Indian word, meaning "dirt space for ceremonial games," and that is what the bar is, an old San Juan home pushing its third century and left in utter disrepair for decades. Regulars claim the jukebox is the best in the Antilles.

Steps and statues: Across Cristo from San Juan Cathedral, between the fork of two of San Juan's oldest and most pleasant *adoquine* streets, lies the lush **Plazuela de las Monjas** (Nun's Square), a perfect spot for an urban picnic. The Square looks out not only on the Cathedral and El Convento, but also the **Casa Cabildo**, San Juan's original City Hall, which now houses a fashionable interior design company.

A walk down **Caleta San Juan** will take you to **San Juan Gate**, constructed in 1939 and the only one of three original portals remaining. Sailors weary of their voyages used to moor their ships in San Juan Bay, ferry themselves ashore, enter through the gates, and walk to prayer services via Caleta San Juan, which describes a conveniently straight line between the gates and the main altar of the Cathedral.

The gates, which were once open to one-way vehicular traffic, now lead to the Paseo la Princesa, a romantic bayfront promenade that skirts the Old City walls. Along this immaculate pedestrian boulevard facing the sea, orderly kiosk vendors sell everything from cotton candy to *guarapo de caña* (sugarcane juice). One dollar gets you an ice-cold glass of the stuff, crushed right before your eyes.

San Juan Bay is considered too polluted to swim in by the local authorities.

The Museo Pablo Casals.

But the more adventurous do often swim to the right of the big pier outside the San Juan gates.

Continuing up Recinto del Oeste past more examples of fine colonial architecture, one reaches a modern sculpture of religious women in procession. This is **La Rogativa** and commemorates the failure of an English siege of San Juan in the spring of 1797. The legend runs that General Sir Ralph Abercromby led a fleet of British ships to take San Juan in a rapid, all-out assault by land and sea. When this plan failed, Abercromby ordered a naval blockade, which lasted two weeks, while the residents of San Juan began to suffer from dysentery, losing hope of the arrival of Spanish reinforcements from the inland settlements. The governor called for a *rogativa*, or divine entreaty, to the Saints Ursula and Catherine. All the women of San Juan marched through the town carrying torches, to the accompaniment of loud ringing of tocsins. Abercromby, believing reinforcements had arrived, quit San Juan never to return.

The walk back to the Cathedral on **Caleta de las Monjas** is full of surprises, chief among them, the stepped streets leading up to the left toward Calles Sol and San Sebastián. At the top of the first, **Escalinata de las Monjas**, is the old Palace of the Bishop of San Juan. The second, **Calle de Hospitál**, detours left around the Palace to San Juan's Hospital Rodríguez. The two streets are somewhat in disrepair, but are the only two of their type that remain in a city that was once full of them.

With all the historical legacy San Juan offers, it's sometimes easy to forget to view the city as its natives view it: as a place to have fun. Calle San Sebastián is perhaps the preeminent place in the old city to do just that. Perpendicular to the top of Calle del Cristo, it's a place of museums and old homes whose many bars and spacious plaza make it a mecca for *sanjuanero* youth of all descriptions from all over the island.

Plaza San José serves as the centerpiece for the street, paved with rosy Spanish conglomerate around a statue

La Rogativa.

of Ponce de León made from English cannons melted down after the first invasion. The plaza draws hundreds of partying teenagers on warm weekend evenings ("evenings" being at about 1am in Puerto Rico) and hundreds of tourists throughout the year.

San Juan's **Dominican Convent** dominates the plaza. Built in 1523, this mammoth, white, elegantly domed structure has seen as much history as any on the island, having housed both English and Dutch occupying forces over the centuries.

The Convent now houses an office of the **Institute of Puerto Rican Culture**, the body which has been more than any other responsible for the renaissance in Puerto Rican scholarship and art over the last several years. Under their auspices, the parts of the convent not used for office space have been converted to cultural ends. A beautiful indoor patio is the scene of many concerts and plays, and now serves as the focus for the magnificent San Juan Museum of History and Art. The old convent

library has been restored to its original 16th-century decor, and the nearby **Center of Popular Arts** offers exposure to local artists.

Museum spin-offs: A whole complex of museums has sprung up around the Dominican convent. The **Museo Pablo Casals**, which abuts the convent, is a petite, gray, two-story townhouse storing memorabilia of the legendary cellist who moved to Puerto Rico in 1957 and lived here until his death in 1973. It includes manuscripts, instruments, texts of his speeches to the United Nations, and a collection of cassettes of his music which can be heard on request. A Casals arts festival takes place every year.

The **Museum of Santos** includes numerous examples of that most Puerto Rican of art forms, *santo*, or "saint" carving. These small, brightly colored wood shapes were used by the early Spanish missionaries to coax the native Taíno Indians of Puerto Rico to convert to Christianity.

Other interesting visits in the Dominican Convent area include the **In-**

Street market in Plaza San José.

dian Museum, the Museum of Pharmacy and the Library of the Society of Puerto Rican Authors.

Next to the Convent itself is the stunning and unusual Church of San José. Built shortly after the convent in the 1530s, San José is the second oldest church in the western hemisphere; only San Juan Cathedral, a half-block down the street, is older. The Gothic architecture of the structure is a true rarity; only the Spanish arrived in the New World early enough to build Gothic churches, and only a handful exist today. The interior of San José certainly has far more charm than that of the nearby cathedral. A wooden crucifix of the mid-16th century, donated by Ponce de León, is one of the highlights here, as is the 15th-century altar brought from Cadíz. The church was the original resting place of Ponce de León in Puerto Rico, after his body was removed from Cuba, and the great Puerto Rican painter, José Campeche, is also buried here.

Across from the Plaza San José is the Cuartel de Ballajá, built as a hospital and later home to Spanish troops and their families. This structure is the centerpiece of Puerto Rico's $100 million effort to restore Old San Juan for the 500th anniversary of Columbus' arrival in the New World, celebrated in 1992. A black granite tablet in Spanish offers maps of the area and tells how the building was restored.

Directly in front is the three-level Plaza del Quinto Centenario which looks out over the Atlantic. Dominating this plaza, at the center of an eight-pointed pavement design, is the Totem Telurico, a terracotta (some say phallic) sculpture by local artist Jaime Suárez that symbolizes the blending of Taíno, African and Spanish cultures. Nearby is a fountain with 100 jets of water; it is supposed to symbolize five centuries of Puerto Rican history.

On Ballajá's second floor is the Museo de las Américas, which provides an overview of cultural development in the New World. Among its colorful exhibit of crafts in the Americas is everything from a replica of a country chapel to an exhibit on Haitian voodoo.

Directly across the plaza from the Cuartel de Ballajá, along unmarked Calle Beneficiencia, is the stately Antiguo Asilo de Beneficienca (Old Home for the Poor). The building was constructed in the 1840s to house the destitute, and today serves as headquarters for the Puerto Rican Institute of Culture. Climb the stairs, go through an ornate foyer and enter the room to your left. Here you'll find an impressive exhibit on the Taínos, and artifacts from the Caguana Indian Ceremonial Park near Utuado and other sites. On your right is a small exhibit of Puerto Rican religious statues. Two huge interior courtyards are used for cultural activities; surrounding them are the institute's main offices.

The Spanish colonists considered San Juan chiefly as a military stronghold, and held military architecture as their first priority. It is not surprising, then, that contemporary *sanjuaneros* are proudest of the breathtaking forts, unique in the western world, that their antecedents left them.

El Morro: El Castillo San Felipe del

eft, San José hurch. ight, view of a Perla and l Morro from an Cristóbal.

Morro, simply known as **El Morro**, the larger of the two forts, commands San Juan Bay with six levels of gun emplacements and walls that tower 140 feet over the Atlantic. Its guns' embrasures were capable of aiming at any ship within El Morro's field of vision, no matter the distance, and the walls themselves, connected with the system that circles San Juan, are 20 feet thick.

The fort's first battery was completed in the 1540s, but it was not until 1589, when Juan Bautista Antonelli arrived with a team of other Spanish military engineers to begin raising a true bulwark along the edge of the peninsula, that the fort was completed. When Sir Francis Drake attacked in 1595, he was roundly repulsed, but Cumberland's land attack from the Condado succeeded in piercing El Morro's still vulnerable rear approach.

The English held the fort for three months until dysentery took the lives of nearly half their men. It would be the last time El Morro would fall, even holding out against the Dutch siege of 1625 and the American gunnery fire which rained upon it during the Spanish-American War of 1898.

Today, visitors appreciate El Morro more for its breathtaking views and architecture than for the protection it affords them. The approach to the fort is over a vast, 27-acre parkland, former drill square for the soldiers and current haven for kite-flyers and strolling lovers. A gravel path through the green leads over a moat and into the massive structure, crossing El Morro's main courtyard, with its beautiful yellow walls and white archways. Here are a souvenir shop and a museum, both of which are useful in orienting the traveler to the fort's layout and history.

The massive archway facing over San Juan Bay on the west side of the courtyard is the entrance to what looks like the longest skateboard run in the world, a huge, stone, step-flanked ramp leading to the lower ramparts, the area of the fort known as the **Santa Barbara Bastion**. This is the most popular of the fort's various sections, affording views

Entrance to E Morro.

of the surf crashing below, and profiling the fort from the ocean side, as its invaders saw it. Definitely not recommended for the agrophobic.

Back upon the upper level of El Morro, a left turn through the courtyard patio leads to another ramp, this one twisting rightwards towards the **Port of San Juan Lighthouse**. This highest point of El Morro was destroyed by an American mortar shell during the Spanish-American War, but later restored, and currently functions to mark the channel entrance to San Juan Harbor.

One note about the lovely rounded sentry boxes that line the walls of San Juan's forts. Known as *garitas*, these are peculiar to the island, and, indeed, serve as the official symbol of the island which they guard. However, they are very secluded, and as San Juan is a city short on public restrooms, they are occasionally quite odoriferous.

San Juan Cemetery, considered by many to be the most picturesque resting-place for old bones in the world, sits on a broad, grassy hummock of land tucked between El Morro's walls and the pounding surf. Its highlight is a tiny circular chapel, set among the bleach-white gravestones and dating from the late 19th century.

Abutting El Morro's grounds, the **Casa Blanca** is the oldest house in Puerto Rico, having been built for Ponce de León in 1521. Used in the years preceding the construction of La Fortaleza as a shelter against the attacks of savage Carib tribes, it was owned by the Ponce family until the late 18th century and now houses the offices of Puerto Rico's Institute for Advanced Studies. The nearby **Casa Rosa** is a lovely pink building overlooking the bay and serves as the office for the Puerto Rican College of Architects.

La Perla: A glance down the beachfront at El Morro will show one the most bizarre and colorful coastal cityscapes imaginable. One- and two-story shacks, seemingly piled one on top of another, crowd the coastline all the way from El Morro to San Cristóbal, running along the battlements which formerly con-

Cemetery, Old San Juan.

nected the two castles. This is **La Perla**, the so-called "world's prettiest slum," which Oscar Lewis immortalized in his study of slum-life, *La Vida*. Set against the backdrop of an aquamarine Atlantic it looks at first glance delightful, but even the toughest of San Juan residents will warn tourists against drugs, violence and a general lawlessness which is rampant in this otherwise charming neighborhood.

Though overshadowed by its more famous neighbor to the west, **El Castillo de San Cristóbal** makes as fascinating a trip as El Morro. What El Morro achieved with brute force, San Cristóbal achieved with subtlety. It sits 150 feet above the waves, reflects the best of 17th-century military architectural thought, and has an intricate network of tunnels that was used both for transporting artillery and for ambushing luckless invaders.

The fort was completed in 1678 as a means of staving off land attacks on San Juan, like the one the Earl of Cumberland had made to capture El Morro in 1595. But the fort as it is known today is the product of the acumen of two Irishmen, "Wild Geese" who had fled from the Orange monarchy and were in the employ of the Spanish army.

Alejandro O'Reilly and Tomas O'Daly designed a system of battlements and sub-forts that ensured that no one could take San Cristóbal without taking all of its ramparts first. No one ever did. The first shot of the Spanish-American War was fired from San Cristóbal's walls. Today the United States Army maintains administrative offices here.

Frequent guided tours explain how San Cristóbal's unique system of defense worked, as well as pointing out some of the fort's big attractions, like the "**Devil's Sentry Box**," a *garita* at the end of a long tunnel that runs to the waterline. Views from the battlements are outstandingly spectacular, particularly in the direction *sanjuaneros* describe as "towards Puerto Rico:" Condado, Hato Rey and El Yunque.

<u>Right</u>, cannonballs at Fort San Cristóbal.

It's easy to try to relegate **Puerta de Tierra** to the status of a sort of verdant buffer zone between San Juan's body and its soul, separating as it does the brawn of Santurce from the historical grandeur and romance of Old San Juan. But Puerto Rico's greatest allure must often be sought out, and so it is with Puerta de Tierra. The word means "gateway of land," but Puerta de Tierra is a gateway in more ways than the narrow literal sense.

Beachfront capitol: Commanding a fabulous view of beach and blue water, straddled by Puerta de Tierra's two main thoroughfares, **El Capitolio**, Puerto Rico's Capitol Building, serves as centerpiece to the whole peninsula. Designed by Puerto Rican architect Rafael Carmoega and constructed between 1925 and 1929, the building is a grand, white classical structure resembling the Capitol building in Washington, on a rather smaller scale, but with wonderful ocean views.

The large rotunda, the last part of the building to be completed, has been stocked with baubles and seals symbolizing the island's history. Highlights include a lovely stained-glass mosaic of Puerto Rico's coat of arms, below which rests the Constitution of Puerto Rico, signed in 1952 and brought back to the island in 1992 after spending nearly five years in a Washington restoration lab.

Nearby are a number of other buildings which, though less imposing, are no less beautiful. The **Casa de España**, just down the hill towards Old San Juan from the Capitolio, rates very high in the esteem of San Juan residents. This blue-tiled, four-towered edifice built in 1935 and paid for by the Spanish expatriate community, lies tucked into hilly greenery between the two main avenues. Once a popular gathering spot for local gentlemen, it now serves as the site for cultural events.

Down Avenida Ponce de León is another lovely edifice, the **Archives and General Library of Puerto Rico**. Pedestals and pilasters support a graceful pediment, and throw a skeleton of white against a lovely sun-washed yellow. Now run by the Institute of Puerto Rican Culture, the General Library lives up to the standards the institute has set for its other buildings, with solemn tessellation of red stone, delicate chandeliers and fine furniture. There's also a peaceful, if small, chapel on the first floor. If this seems out of place in a national library, it is because the building, built in 1877 as the last major Spanish architectural effort on the island, was originally designed as a hospital.

Other important landmarks along the boulevard towards Condado include the headquarters of the Popular Democratic Party, the **Puerto Rico National Guard Armory** and **Parque Luis Muñoz Rivera**, with its Peace Pavilion dedicated in 1991 by Nobel Peace Prize winner and former Costa Rican President Oscar Arias.

The **Caribe Hilton** sits on several acres of beautifully landscaped grass and sand, overlooking a little beach-

lined cove that stretches to Condado. The pool is inviting, never overcrowded, and overlooked by a lavishly accoutred bar with *piña coladas* so good you wish you could stay inside all day and drink.

But the Caribe also has a historical asset in **Fort San Gerónimo**, a small but crucial element of the old Spanish fortifications which stymied a British invasion in 1797. The military museum inside is entertaining and worthwhile.

Condado: "Condado" in Spanish means "county," and many Puerto Ricans still refer to the glittering strip of land between the Condado lagoon and Atlantic Ocean as "*the* Condado." If the appellation is meant to convey anything rustic or sleepy about this part of town, it grossly misses the mark. A trip across the Puente San Gerónimo from Puerta de Tierra takes one out of history and into hysteria, into a world where gambling, dining, drinking and dancing are the life of the night, a world where conspicuous wealth and a hectic North American lifestyle are *de rigueur*.

Ashford Avenue, Condado's main thoroughfare, looks as though it is desperately trying to run for election as the sixth borough of New York, or perhaps as an annex of Miami Beach. In a large measure, it succeeds. Its miles of beachfront are lined with chic boutiques, banks, restaurants and – most conspicuously – hotels.

Hotels are, of course, of varying quality in Condado, but the town's lodgings seldom dip very far below the "luxury" rating. Many have casinos, and most of the casinos require ties. The casinos aren't exclusive; non-hotel patrons are welcome at the tables, as long as they bring their wallets. Restaurants, both hotel-affiliated and otherwise, tend to be of good quality. There's a price to pay for quality in Condado, and it is a high one. Some of the restaurants in town are almost legendary but worth it for the experience.

Restaurants with class: La Brasserie offers some of the finest French cooking found anywhere in the Caribbean; the **Scotch and Sirloin**, with its hefty portions, quiet outdoor tables and breathtaking view ("The only thing we overlooked," runs one advertisement, "is the lagoon."); the **Chart House**, in what seems a miracle, gathers an immensely diverse collection of seafood from Alaska to Venezuela under the roof of a lovely three-story townhouse.

To go to the beach in Condado implies more than taking the sun and riding the waves. (The surf, by the way, is positively uninspiring compared to that in Rincón and Jobos.) Here, people-watching is the chief popular pastime, and there is certainly a fine variety to watch. The beach itself is decent, but, as with the surf, there is better to be had. The sand, lovely and white, is strewn hither and thither with gum wrappers and empty suntan lotion bottles; the water is warm and unpolluted. The Condado strip of sand, by the way, is the first beach east of San Juan which the Department of Natural Resources considers "swimmable." One unfortunate consideration for swimming and body-watching buffs who are just visiting Condado and don't have hotel rooms is that the wall of hotels lining the beach

Sunning on Condado Beach.

has made access somewhat difficult in spots. Remember that none of the beachfront is privately owned – all the beaches in Puerto Rico are public – but the big hotels aren't going to go out of their way to show anyone the easy route to the beach. The determined visitor, of course, will usually find the way.

Ocean Park: Heading east on Ashford Avenue, past the Burger King and the Citibank on the right and the Ambassador Plaza on the left, one approaches **Ocean Park**, Condado's wild and woolly western fringe. Here, the houses become smaller and more spread out, and the beaches grow less crowded, but the ambience does not become any less American.

This is one of the more scenic of San Juan's beachfront panoramas, with views stretching from the palm-lined point at Boca de Cangrejos to the bright-white high-rise wall of Ashford Avenue's hotels. After a swim and perhaps a look at one of the longest and most varied stretches of Puerto Rico's north coast, retire to **Kasalta's**, an oasis of

fine native cuisine in a desert of kitsch. Here you'll find all the San Juan newspapers, a range of Puerto Rican delicacies unmatched on the island, and a fresh cup of native coffee that will electrify you.

South of Condado: A knot of highways and main roads, **Santurce** connects the more touristed and, admittedly, more picturesque areas of the metropolis. It can't claim a seacoast; in fact, one could almost define the area as the set of neighborhoods one encounters moving south from more fashionable Condado and Ocean Park. It hasn't the history of Old San Juan, having been founded only about a century ago as a fashionable suburb. But Santurce does have manifold charms of its own, making it well worth a visit for those few who are prepared to make the effort.

Love, not money: Santurce is considered by most to be the heart of San Juan, and not just in the sense that it's the source of the city's main traffic arteries. At a time when most world cities have razed their most charming business dis-

tricts, Santurce survives as a true marketplace. The quaintest manifestation of this ethic is in the **Santurce Market** on Calle Canals, where vendors bargain and sell in much the same way as in the more renowned market in Río Piedras.

While many *sanjuaneros* come to work in Santurce, a surprising proportion come to eat. The area has long been host to many of the island's most elegant restaurants, but its most appealing establishments are often little *fondas*, as low on price as they are on pretentiousness. The arts thrive in Santurce as well, and the construction in 1981 of the **Centro de Bellas Artes**, at the corner of Avenidas Ponce de Léon and José de Diego, has brought the neighborhood a new share in San Juan's cultural wealth. Old movie buffs have long known that Santurce is practically the only locale in which to take in a good flick.

Back on the western edge of Santurce, closest to Old San Juan, is **Miramar**, one of the most charming and paradoxical of the suburbs in the metropolitan area where lovely tree-lined avenues of pretty modern residences abut one of the island's sleazier red-light districts.

Airport beach: Almost everyone arrives in Puerto Rico at Luís Muñoz Marín International Airport in **Isla Verde**. Technically part of the municipality of Carolina, this San Juan suburb takes on a look of affluence that few areas as close to such booming noise, annoying traffic snarls and transient lifestyle possess – big, chalk-white blocks of high-income apartment houses choke one of the most beautiful beachfronts on the island, giving Isla Verde one of the most Miami-Beachesque aspects this side of… well, Miami Beach.

Isla Verde is very rich, but hardly anyone in Puerto Rico would disagree that it has never quite got over being an airport town. It's a bit dull. The usual airport businesses – car rental agencies, vinyl cocktail lounges and the like – have overrun the place, and most of the residents of the area are either retired or doing their best to pretend they are. Part of the problem is, of course, location; suburbs separate Isla Verde from the **Isla Verde.**

historical charms of the older parts of San Juan, while water separates it from the charms of Piñones.

Riding the waves: This is not, however, to count Isla Verde as being utterly without its charms. **Playas Punta las Marias** and **Isla Verde** stretch for over a mile of white sand from the end of the beach at Ocean Park to the lovely coral reefs at Boca de Cangrejos. The surf here is formidable, especially in winter, and the area known as **Piñones** is among the most popular hangouts for young people throughout the year. And when the surf is up, and young bodies are working up a thirst riding the waves, those huge white hotels can seem very welcoming indeed.

Hato Rey: It's odd that in so many of the great cities of the world, financial brawn and bohemian asceticism have shared the same neighborhoods. Opposites attract: New York's arty districts of Tribeca and Soho rub shoulders with Wall Street: London's City is surrounded by universities and galleries. San Juan follows this rule to an unusual degree.

Here, **Hato Rey**, the undisputed business and high-finance capital of the Caribbean, abuts – and often intermingles with – **Río Piedras**, the home of the University of Puerto Rico.

The Golden Mile: Most of the money in the Antilles is filtered through a group of institutions clustered on a section of Expreso Luís Muñoz Rivera in Hato Rey known as the **Golden Mile**. Though Operation Bootstrap certainly contributed to Puerto Rico's importance as a financial center, the recent emergence of Hato Rey as a mecca for banks and Section 936 corporations owes a great deal to a long-standing Puerto Rican commitment to banking. Here, some $8 billion in profits generated by the "936 firms" are kept on deposit.

Not everyone comes to San Juan to make a buck, but everyone who visits should head down to Hato Rey nonetheless, if only to see the intriguing modern architecture banking always seem to drag in its wake. Particularly interesting is the **Banco de Santander Building** – which, with its reflecting plate-glass

Hato Rey and Río Piedras.

arching from an austere concrete shaft, looks something like a giant refrigerator. Hato Rey is also the headquarters of **Banco Popular de Puerto Rico**, which is the island's oldest and largest bank. In 1993, Banco Popular celebrated its 100th anniversary.

Enrique Adsuar González, a respected commentator on local custom, has mentioned that the sight of Hato Rey businessmen walking the streets in Wall Street-cut woollen winter suits in 90-degree weather is one of the great ironies of contemporary Puerto Rican life.

Hato Rey has also become something of a culinary capital, if in a modest and basic way. One can't expect gourmet food in restaurants which cater solely to men who will lose their jobs if they go for an extra course, but solid Puerto Rican fare is to be had here for prices one wouldn't mind paying in the Cordillera.

A mile west of the business district on Route 23 (Avenida Franklin Delano Roosevelt) are two of Puerto Rico's more adventurous recent structures. The first, on the north side of the highway, is **Plaza de las Américas,** a real *norteamericano* shopping mall with fountains and flowered walks, where locals flock to buy everything from *guayaberas* (shirts) to guava juice. Across the highway to the south is the **Estadio Hiram Bithorn**, an odd, hyper-modern Puerto Rican stadium, which is the site for a variety of sporting and cultural events.

Río Piedras: Perhaps Hato Rey maintains its humanity due only to the humanizing influence of the university town of Río Piedras to the south. Within the shortest of walks, concrete and plate glass give way to cobbled paths and flower gardens. With its 25,000 students and distinguished faculty from all parts of Latin America, the **University of Puerto Rico** is certainly unique in the American university community. Among those who've taught here have been Juan Ramón Jiménez, Pablo Casals and Arturo Morales Carrión. The Jiménez Room, located on campus, contains a large collection of the poet's personal effects. The octagonal clock-

Roberto Clemente Stadium, Hato Rey.

tower, which soars out of the palms at one side of the campus, has become something of a symbol for Río Piedras.

The highlight of any visit to Río Piedras, however, must be the **Botanical Gardens** at the Agricultural Experimental Station a mile south of the university and reachable by following the signs after turning off at the intersection of Muñoz Rivera and Route 847. Hundreds of varieties of tropical and semitropical plants, including many from Australia and Africa, make up one of the most extensive parks of its type in the world. The gardens will comprise 200 acres (80 hectares) when completed. Suffice it to say that it's hard to imagine a botanical garden landscaped as imaginatively or as subtly as this one. Ponds, lilies, ferns and ubiquitous *yautía* compete for attention with a lush, disorderly orchid garden.

Río Piedras is not, however, all ivory towers and ivied lanes. Its **Paseo de Diego** is the largest pedestrian market in San Juan, with all the haggling, gesticulation and frenzy of an Arab *souk*. This is the place to go if you'd like a cultural education.

In fact, only four blocks away from the main plaza is the neighborhood's most interesting street, **Calle Padre Colón** – heart of Puerto Rico's small but vibrant Arab community. Most of the community's 2,000 or so members are Palestinians whose families came here in the 1950s as street vendors and clothing merchants. On this street, storefronts display such names as Khami Rabi, Suleiman Imports and Jerusalem Inc. The Islamic Center of Puerto Rico, also located here, has main prayers every Friday.

For a real lunch or dinner treat, try the **Middle East Restaurant**, where you can find homemade appetizers such as *humus* with *tehini* sauce, *felafel* or *tabouli* salad. For a more extensive Arab meal, ask for the *shishkebab* platter or *cordero relleno* (whole lamb with rice, pistachio nuts, garnishing and salad). Finish it all off with a traditional cup of *kawfie hal* (cardamom coffee) and sweet *baklava* for dessert.

Below left, the Botanical Gardens. Below right, the university clocktower.

CATAÑO AND BAYAMÓN

Crossing from San Juan on the Cataño Ferry allows excellent views of wind-swept San Juan Bay. **Cataño** itself is by no means a picturesque town. It is hap-hazard, almost shadeless, and utterly without charm in its shopping areas. It does, however, have a beachfront area and unrivaled views of Old San Juan.

A rum affair: In the most remote cor-ners of the world, people who have no idea where Puerto Rico is nevertheless know the name Bacardí. That they auto-matically associate it with Puerto Rico is all the more surprising, considering that Bacardí isn't the island's only rum, or even its best. Yet few tourists visit Puerto Rico without making the almost obligatory pilgrimage to the sprawling **Bacardí Rum Plant**, 5 minutes west on Route 165, which distils millions of gallons yearly, and offers free tours in bizarre little two-coach trolley buses. There, they sip free piña coladas while

looking out over San Juan Bay, and buy bottles of rum to lug back home.

All this would have made the compa-ny's Cuban founder, Don Facundo Bacardí y Maso, very happy. In 1862, Don Facundo distilled his very first bot-tle of rum in Santiago de Cuba. Business was so good that he quickly expanded; by 1936, the Bacardí family decided to open a distillery in Puerto Rico.

In 1959, Fidel Castro came to power in Cuba. Shortly after, the Communists confiscated the family's extensive hold-ings – worth an estimated $76 million at the time – and the Bacardís were forced to shift production to Puerto Rico, Ber-muda, the Bahamas and elsewhere.

Today, Bacardí, the world's number one spirit, is truly a global empire, with plants in more than a dozen countries. Through a web of companies that in-clude Bacardí Corp., Bacardí & Co., Bacardí Ltd and half a dozen others, the empire now accounts for 75 percent of United States and 50 percent of all world rum consumption, with more than seven million cases sold every year.

Throughout its long history, Bacardí has also produced its share of family feuds. In 1988, a battle erupted between majority stockholders who wanted to privatize Bacardí Corp., and executive vice-president Adolfo Comas Bacardí, who wanted it to remain public. Comas lost, and today he's administrator of the island's largest newspaper, *El Nuevo Día*. In the meantime, Bacardí Corp. alone enjoys sales of around $400 mil-lion a year and pays half that amount in federal liquor excise taxes.

The company offers free bilingual tours of its Cataño distillery every 20 minutes (Monday–Saturday, 9–10.30am and 12–4pm, though it's best to go on a weekday in order to see the bottling line in production). The tour begins on the first floor, then up to the fifth floor for an exhibit of Bacardí products, and finally down to the second floor, where the production process is explained.

From the distillery – which has a capacity of 100,000 gallons a day – tourists are taken by trolley to the Bacardí family museum, and finally to the visi-tor's pavilion, where free piña coladas

The world's number one spirit.

are waiting. Here on the spacious Bacardí grounds, looking across the bay to Old San Juan, is the site of the two-week Bacardí Arts Festival every December.

Some locals worry that once Fidel Castro is gone, the Cuban economy will suddenly open up, allowing Bacardí to reclaim its confiscated property and move its base of operations back to Cuba. But in reality, the company's departure from Puerto Rico is very unlikely. Federal rum-tax rebates make the island an enviable manufacturing site, not to mention easy market access to the mainland and political stability under the American flag.

Seafood center: Bathed in the warm aroma of Bacardí's molasses, **Palo Seco**, though not in Cataño proper, lures most of Cataño's visitors with its seafood. An almost unbroken string of restaurants, many named after local pirate Roberto Confresí, runs parallel to the ocean.

At the end of a pine-flecked spit of land is **Isla de Cabras**, now a recreational area and hangout for local fishermen. The island originally housed the long-range artillery of **Fort Cañuelo**, built in 1608. In later centuries, it served as a leper colony. Cabras also boasts a beautiful – but unswimmable – beach. Hedonists should head further west on Route 165; across Ensenada de Boca Vieja, **Punta Salinas** is flanked by two of the prettiest beaches in the area.

Cowboy town: To the south of Cataño is **Bayamon** whose inhabitants are referred to as *vaqueros* or "cowboys." This is due to a sort of maverick quality that has put the city in friendly opposition to others on the island.

Founded in 1509 by a group of settlers led by Ponce de León, Bayamon labors under the stereotype of a sort of glorified shopping mall. It is a place where the antiquated *fincas* and plantations of an older Puerto Rico are set in sharp juxtaposition to some of the most innovative civic architecture. Bayamon has been fastidious about retaining its regional customs and cuisine. Along almost every road leading into the city are *bayamonés* food vendors selling roast chicken, bread, and the most legendary of all local treats – the *chicharrón*, a tart

mix of pork and spice baked into a tough, bread mass. Male visitors should know that *chicharrón* has a connotation which makes it inadvisable to ask local women if they would like to taste.

Bayamon's first sight is the eight-story **Alcaldía de Bayamon**, which spans five lanes of highway. Built in 1978 of concrete, glass, and lemon-yellow steel I-beams, it is the only building so suspended in the Caribbean.

Across the highway is the **Estadio Juan Ramón Loubriel**, an attractive modern baseball stadium. On the same side of the highway, the **Parque Central** is also dedicated to recreation, with historical and cultural displays including an airplane and an old locomotive. Nearby, in the placid **Paseo Barbosa** numerous shops are ranged about the restored 19th-century house of Barbosa.

Bayamon native Francisco Oller was Puerto Rico's greatest artist; his work is at the **Museo Francisco Oller** in the Old Alcaldía at Calle Degetau, 2. And there is the impressive science museum, the **Parque de Ciencias**.

Antique locomotive in Bayamon's Parque Central.

THE NORTHEAST AND THE ISLANDS

If someone arriving in Puerto Rico with the inexcusable intention of spending only a few days here were to hire a guide and ask to be shown as much as possible of the island, he would be driven directly east from San Juan. It is not that the northeastern corner of the island contains all the island's attractions; that would be impossible. It is only that the variety of landscapes and societies – none of them farther than 45 minutes from San Juan – is mind-boggling. The ease with which one can move from one landscape to another which bears no resemblance to the previous one will make even the crassest traveler feel he is cheating.

The palm groves and beachside settlements of Boca de Cangrejos are visible from San Juan, but a world apart. Mysterious Loíza takes you across an ocean and an eon to a world of African society and ritual. Towering El Yunque dominates the only rain forest in the National Park system, and Luquillo, almost in its shadow, guards what is perhaps Puerto Rico's finest beach.

From Fajardo, a preeminent sailor's haven, ferries depart for Vieques and Culebra, two idyllic Lesser Antillean isles that belong to Puerto Rico only politically. Here the attractions are great beaches, spectacular diving, and an intangible sense of adventure. Returning to the main island from Vieques and Culebra without a handful of colorful anecdotes and a host of new friends is not easy; in fact, returning to the main island is not easy at all.

Preceding pages: setting moon over El Yunque; loading plantains. **Left**, horsing around in Boca de Cangrejos.

BEACHES AND OFFSHORE CAYS

Puerto Rico is full of surprises at every bend of the road, but nowhere are the island's contrasts more shocking than on Route 187 just east of San Juan. Here, the highway that links the metropolis with the Caribbean's most modern international airport passes over a bridge and turns into a rutted, barely navigable path through Edenic palm groves, herds of bony Puerto Rican cows and sheep and a cluster of ramshackle lean-tos running the length of the beach.

This is **Boca de Cangrejos** ("Crab-mouth"), as exotic a spot as one will find within 20 minutes of any major city in the world. It is at first appearance perhaps Puerto Rico at its most typically Latin American (read "Third World"), but the ricketiness is deceptive. The flocks belong to the residents of nearby settlements around the *municipio* of Loíza. The shacks are not residences by any stretch of the imagination, rather beachfront food emporia unrivaled by any on the island, save perhaps those at Luquillo. Boca de Cangrejos is where *sanjuaneros* retreat for a *coco frío* – ice cold coconut milk which is served in its own shell.

Grove diggers: Long beaches under luxuriant pine groves are what draw visitors to Boca de Cangrejos. Surfers are the most devoted of such partisans, and can be seen riding the waves at the part of the beach called **Los Aviones** ("The Airplanes") after the flights from Isla Verde that roar over all day.

It's commonly advised to stay away from **Piñones** when the beach is deserted, which seldom happens. Those who crave company, tend to stick to the extreme eastern and western ends of the beach, where the finest views of the Santurce skyline are to be had.

Piñones grows more eerie, rustic and beautiful as one moves east. At its farthest point from San Juan is **Vacia Talega Beach**, a breathtaking finger of rock capped by palms and carved into strange formations by eons of surf.

Beach at Boca de Cangrejos.

Beyond the swamps: Few towns in Puerto Rico balance natural beauty and cultural achievement as gracefully or as charmingly as Loíza Aldea. Just 6 miles east of metropolitan San Juan, predominantly black **Loíza** (population 29,000), has maintained its separateness from the capital thanks to a cluster of natural barriers. Puerto Rico's largest mangrove swamp, the massive and mysterious woodland of **Torrecilla Baja**, sits smack between the two communities, and can be traversed only via the rutted coastal Route 187, which goes through Piñones and crosses the **Río Grande de Loíza**, Puerto Rico's widest, roughest, and only navigable river.

Loíza is arguably among the purest centers of true African culture in the western world. It was settled in the 16th century by black slaves sent by the Spanish crown to mine a rich gold deposit in the area. When the gold ran out, they became cane-cutters and, when slavery was abolished in 1873, many blacks turned to this agricultural economy.

They learned Spanish and became Catholics, but in the subsequent fusion of African culture with Spanish and Indian, the African certainly won out. Such influence is most visible during the Fiesta de Santiago Apostól, when the people of Loíza gather to praise Saint James, patron of the town. The week-long celebration commences each July 25, when citizens dress in ceremonial costumes strikingly and significantly similar to those of the Yoruba tribe of West Africa, from whom many of Puerto Rico's blacks are descended. Participants include masqueraders, ghouls and *viejos* (old men), and the making of costumes for the ceremonial rites is ordered by a social hierarchy which is quite alien to Latin America.

The most distinctive festival attire, however, belongs to the *veigantes*, most of them young men, who dress in garish costumes and parade through the streets. Their religious purpose is generally taken to be that of frightening the lapsed back into the Christian faith, though they can be just as much a source of celebration and mirth. Most true *veigante*

Mask maker in Loíza.

masks are made from coconuts or other gourds carved into grimaces like those of the most sinister jack-o-lanterns. At times aluminum foil is used to make the mask's teeth look even more eerie.

The best beach: There's plenty to see in Puerto Rico's northeast, but few informed visitors get to see any of the area's attractions without first making at least a day's detour to what many consider the island's finest beach. Shimmering **Luquillo** is just 35 minutes west of San Juan on Route 3, which, in travelers' terms, is about the same time it would take one to get to lovely but arduous El Yunque or Fajardo's mob scene, and about half the time it would take to get to grisly Humacao. The only liability of a trip to Luquillo is that it is overcrowded, especially at weekends.

Mountains to the sea: Even those not terribly enthusiastic about beaching will find it hard to ignore Luquillo's appeal. This beautiful, bleach-white town is tucked cozily between dark Atlantic waters and Puerto Rico's most imposing mountain chain, the Sierra de Luquillo, from which the town draws its name. There are few more dramatic sights on the island than that of the whitecaps of the shoreline glistening in summer sunlight while the peaks of the El Yunque rain forest just inland are suffused in purple thunder clouds. Occasionally, some of the rain intended for the forest does fall on Luquillo, and quite often the beach is under heavy cloud cover.

Luquillo is listed officially as being 2¼ miles long but it's linked to two other swimmable beaches – **Playas San Miguel** and **Convento** – which are every bit as lovely and almost deserted, and stretch nearly to Cabezas de San Juan, at the far northeastern end of the island, making ideal walking territory.

Luquillo is also the premier beachside food emporium on Puerto Rico; a seemingly endless string of kiosks – numbered from one to 65 – sells delectably rich local seafood specialties and a variety of hard and non-alcoholic drinks, including the immensely popular *coco frío*, ice-cold coconut milk served in its

Puerto Rico's finest beach, Luquillo.

own shell. There's nothing better to indulge in on a sunny day.

Two-faced town: To some, the town of **Fajardo**, the next sizeable destination beyond Luquillo, is merely an over-cluttered dockfront town, ranking third behind Brindisi, Italy and Hyannis, Massachusetts in the "Grim Ferry Ports of the World." To others it is an eminently glamorous resort, a charming community, gateway to a handful of fabulous islands and home of the finest sailing in the Caribbean.

The first major town along Puerto Rico's northeast coast, Fajardo remains a mecca for yachting enthusiasts. Originally a small fishing and agricultural village, it became in the late 1700s a popular supply port for many pirate and contraband vessels. The town itself, a hodge-podge of clothing, furniture, and video stores, will appear somewhat unprepossessing to most visitors compared to the area's natural attractions – the calm, clear waters and cays and coral reefs of Vieques Sound.

Playa de Fajardo, a waterfront community at the east end of town, docks the ferries headed to Culebra, Vieques and a small island marina nearby. Next to the ferry terminal is the pink stucco **US Post Office/Customs House** and one of Fajardo's few hotels.

Just north of Fajardo, two condominium high-rises, architectural anomalies here, loom over the small fishing village of **Playa Sardinera**. Hundreds of fancy motorboats and yachts of all descriptions crowd the two waterfront marinas nearby. Local fishermen line the beach in the middle of the village with boats and tents; they supply the half dozen expensive little seafood restaurants in the area.

A road over the hill passes a comfortable guesthouse and the lavish **El Conquistador Resort & Country Club**, re-opened in 1993 after a $250 million facelift. With 917 rooms and more than 2,000 employees, El Conquistador is now Puerto Rico's largest resort. It's also one of the most expensive.

The resort, first built in 1960s, was abandoned at one point and later turned

Fajardo.

into a Maharishi university that soon went bankrupt. Today's resort is spread among five distinct themed areas, with Moorish and Spanish architecture featured throughout. Guests can even take a ferry to Palomino Island, where the hotel maintains its own private beach and grill.

The road continues on to **Playa Soroco**, a long, narrow stretch of crisp white-sand beach whose clean, shallow waters make it a favorite among locals. At the leftmost point of Soroco, a dirt road leads to **Playa El Convento**, an isolated beach stretching for miles.

Nearby, right off Route 987, is the **Cabezas de San Juan Nature Preserve**, an environmental paradise that encompasses 316 acres of some of the Caribbean's most stunning landscape. Admission to the preserve is by guided tour only.

Considering the park's beauty, it's surprising that so few tourists have taken the time to explore it since the park's opening in April 1991. Here, one can observe nearly all of Puerto Rico's natural habitats – coral reefs, thalassia beds, sandy and rocky beaches, lagoons, a dry forest and a mangrove forest.

Another important attraction at **Cabezas de San Juan** is the lighthouse, known simply as "El Faro." Built in 1880, this pristine white neoclassical structure with black trim is one of only two operational lighthouses on the island. The view from the Cabezas de San Juan is head-spinning. As you look back towards the heart of Puerto Rico, El Yunque's formidable mountain rain forest towers over the island. In the other direction a chain of cays ranges like enticing stepping stones to the isles of Culebra and Saint Thomas.

The dozens of cays and islands off Fajardo provide Puerto Rico's best boating. A protective reef stretching from Cabezas de San Juan to Culebra and beyond keeps the waters calm, while swift Atlantic tradewinds make for great sailing. Charter a yacht from one of Fajardo's marinas and spend the day sailing, sunbathing and snorkeling.

Icacos, the largest and most popular cay, offers a narrow stretch of bone-white beach, making it a nice spot for picnicking or even camping. Two rows of wood posts from an abandoned dock march into the water, and, just beyond, a coral underworld descends to the sandy bottom 20 feet below. The beach is certainly warm and comfortable, but all the action is around the reefs: elkhorn, staghorn, brain, star, and other corals host legions of underwater plant and animal life.

Other popular cays, somewhat less readily accessible, include **Culebrita,** and **Cayos Lobos** (wolves), **Diablo** (devil), **Palominos** (doves) and **Palominitos** (take a wild guess). These and many smaller cays are ripe for underwater exploration among coral, caverns and tunnels.

Just south of Fajardo, one of the largest naval bases in the world, **Roosevelt Roads**, occupies about a quarter of Puerto Rico's eastern coastline. Headquarters of the US Caribbean Naval Forces, the base fuels all American and Allied ships in the area and oversees large-scale sea maneuvers.

The area around Fajardo is famous for boating.

THE NORTHWEST

Visitors to Puerto Rico may be confounded by the dazzling array of holiday choices that confront them: the neon of San Juan or the phosphorescence of Parguera? The waters at Coamo or Culebra? Cabo Rojo or Cabo San Juan Lighthouse? Other questions are more easily answered, however, and "Where would I choose to live?" frequently elicits "The Northwest" as a response. In this region are some of the island's loveliest and most historical cities – Arecibo, Lares, San Sebastián, Isabela – with all the bustle of San Juan and none of its mind-bending frenzy, all the calm of the Cordillera and none of its backwardness.

To the connoisseur of natural beauty, the northwest is also the most rewarding area of the island, owing to magnificent ranges of karstic *mogotes*, or limestone hillocks, whose likes are found only in a handful of places in the world. Limestone is carved with a master's hand as well in the lovely caves and sinkholes that pepper the whole karstic region. This is beauty on a human scale, true adventurer's territory. And if you're a mush-for-brains *gringo* surfie to whom "beauty on a human scale" means next to nothing, rest assured that the island's best surf is never more than a right turn away on Route 2 anywhere from Arecibo to Mayagüez.

Preceding pages: Some for the road; Sun Bay Beach, Vieques. **Left**, one of Puerto Rico's delectable pineapples.

Driving west from San Juan on Route 2, the landscape opens up a bit, the first hills begin to rise, and the first-time visitor may begin to feel he's left the metropolis and is about to penetrate Puerto Rico's fabled countryside. That is, until he hits sprawling, congested Bayamón; then he begins to wonder if the big cities will ever stop. They stop in **Dorado**, 10 miles west of San Juan, the first town which can claim to be out from under its shadow.

Dorado's a pleasant, quiet, unassuming little town. You'll miss it if you stay on the highway, and may have to look twice for it even if you should take the detour on Route 165, which leaves Route 2 and runs north across emerald marshlands before looping back to Dorado. The town introduces itself well, as they say in the wine trade.

The hospitable hamlet of **Toa Baja** signals the turnoff. If Dorado is unassuming, Toa Baja is positively diffident, though it is full of charms which belie the quiet. Dividing Toa Baja from Dorado itself is the sluggish **Río de la Plata**, whose grassy banks and meandering course would remind you of some of the more timeless parts of rural England were it not for the clayey, river bed which has turned the stream's waters a rugged brick red.

Dorado follows 165 loosely on both sides. No cross streets slow traffic enough to draw attention to the small main plaza by the roadside, and the town's businesses are admirably free of gaudy billboards and other welcome bric-a-brac. "Urban" Dorado is just clean, slow-paced, and friendly, and a disproportionate number of its business establishments – bakeries, bars, juice stands – have camaraderie as their *raison d'être*.

Concrete arrives: What do you do with an unspoiled beach? Spoil it, of course. About two decades ago, Dorado looked like the prime place on a burgeoning tourist island to develop a resort and make a killing. The Rockefeller family decided to develop a few dozen acres of beachfront Dorado landscape and turn it into a luxury sunspot in the manner of Humacao's Palmas del Mar. There's little to be said about the beautifully landscaped and luxuriously accoutred grounds of the Hyatt Regency Cerromar Beach hotel; if you're an ordinary tourist you'll never get near it anyway but it is as relaxing and idyllic as any in the Caribbean.

Dorado boasts an ancient castle, the **Casa del Rey**, whose structure has been restored and converted to government offices. Its residents included Don Lopez Canino, and it will soon be converted into a museum, as Don Lopez and his wife were good to all classes. Illustrious Puerto Ricans who spent time there included José Celso Barbosa, José de Diego and others.

But Dorado is not all culture. Its beaches are inviting and easily accessible via the *guaguas* (buses) that leave from near the town plaza. A mile northwest of town, through a spinney of mangroves and a bone-white graveyard on

Left, petroleum refinery, near Manatí. Right, Cerromar Beach Hotel, Dorado.

Route 693, is the irresistibly lovely beach at **Playa Sardinera**.

Popular beachfront: Further west, a fast, 35-minute drive from San Juan on Routes 2 and 686, **Vega Baja** is one of the most popular of San Juan's metropolitan beachfronts, and benefits not only from spectacular juxtapositions of sand and sea, but from lush and unusual surrounding countryside as well. The beach itself draws most attention for its weird and haunting rock formations. It runs for 2,500 feet from the snug, palm-lined cove of **Boca del Cibuco** to craggy **Punta Puerto Nuevo**.

At Puerto Nuevo a line of coral islands runs parallel to the seashore and meets a rocky headland tangentially. This odd, almost unique formation has sheltered most of Vega Baja while causing its western end to resemble at times a sort of preternaturally large jacuzzi. Further along, and accessible by Route 686 where it runs by the base, is **Puerto del Tortuguero**, the largest and most palm-lined of the beaches. Half a mile inland, **Laguna Tortuguero**, while not officially a nature reserve, provides a haven for bird life.

Foliage and joviality: The town of Vega Baja has grown into a fairly modern and uniform Puerto Rican municipality; new settlements like **La Trocha** and **Pugnado Alfuera** are worth passing through only if you are on your way to the Cordillera. The town does have a sense of humor about its reputation as something of a hokey place. An official town bulletin offers not only the usual information on town history and famous residents, but a tongue-in-cheek roster of *Personajes típicos de Vega Baja*. These include the tallest man, the drunk, the beggar and the basketball fan.

A town that can parody itself so remorselessly deserves a visit, but not so much as the surrounding countryside. Vega Baja sits in the middle of the fertile coastal flatlands west of San Juan. Visitors will be rewarded with long vistas over canefields and marshes, and an array of deciduous foliage most impressive in an island full of tropical trees.

<u>Right</u>, Caribbean sunset.

ARECIBO

There are prettier cities on this island, but few are prettier to approach than **Arecibo**. Forty-eight miles west of San Juan, Route 2 takes a tortuous turn and reveals the second capital city of Puerto Rico's north coast backed by the blue Atlantic. Directly to the south of Arecibo lies the karst country (dealt with in another chapter) with classic karst landscapes of pine and mahogany in the Río Abajo forest.

The coastal road, Route 681, affords an even more dramatic perspective. This is in itself one of the most spectacular drives in Puerto Rico, running from Palmas Altas through Islote, past Desvio Valdes, through a settlement at Punta Caracoles, and by the big radio antennae of the Arecibo station WCMN, before hitting the bay at Puerto de Arecibo. Here you will meet the city in truly spectacular fashion. Middle-sized apartment blocks and business premises seem to loom large and blue across an even bluer bay, and Arecibo takes on something of the air of a western Puerto Rican Eldorado.

The reality of Arecibo is a bit more worldly than you would assume from its externally Arcadian aspect. It's one of the oldest of Puerto Rican towns, and since its foundation in the 16th century has enjoyed one of the highest levels of prosperity on the island.

Operation Bootstrap, the project which was designed by Muñoz Marín and the US Congress to boost Puerto Rico into the industrial world, and Section 936, the American legislation which has offered tax incentives to companies investing in Puerto Rico, have accelerated Arecibo's advance in the business world. Puerto Rico produces more pharmaceutical products than any other place in the world, and Arecibo lies at the center of the pharmaceutical manufacturing industry.

Oil for the wheels of life: Arecibo has

Right, doing the grocery shopping in an Arecibo market.

been a leader in the art of manufacturing products that ease one along the troubled road of life since long before the pharmaceutical boom. Ronrico, one the great rums of the island which is itself the rum capital of the world, is probably the major industry in town. It's hardly the greatest, but it's eminently drinkable, and Arecibo is proud of its part in the island's rum trade.

Arecibo's Chamber of Commerce even goes so far as to acquaint the tourist with the whimsical saga of Don Juan Piza Bisbal, the Catalán who left Barcelona *"con lágrimas en los ojos"* ("with tears in his eyes") to come to Puerto Rico and introduce to Westerners *Ron Llave*, "the key to happiness." Those visitors who have toured the Ronrico plant tend to agree with this appraisal of the salubrious properties of Puerto Rican libations.

Salubrious surroundings: For a town so situated, Arecibo is center to a surprising variety of terrain. It forms a north-easterly pointing semi-peninsula at the delta of two rivers: the **Rio Grande de Arecibo** and the **Canal Perdomo**. To its east recede swamps of unmeasured depth and gloom. This is why the roads from San Juan hug the shoreline to give such pleasant views of the city from afar. *O! Felix culpa!* But not too *felix...* be warned that the surrounding area is chock-a-block with mosquitoes in the wet season.

Arecibo itself disappoints some tourists who use the city as a way station on their ineluctable search for all that is mundane and tacky on the island. It takes an intelligent and observant traveler to realize that Arecibo is one of the finer and more livable cities, not only on the island, but anywhere in the Caribbean. Its streets are broad, its citizens relatively well-off, and its shopping district has far more variety than one might expect from a city of only 75,000 inhabitants.

Moreover, Arecibo has cafes and theaters – not as commonplace as one might think in Puerto Rico – and its oldest, a distinctive wooden structure, dates from 1884. **Calle Alejandro Salicrup**, at the tip of the semi-peninsu-

lar wedge, is one of the best thoroughfares on which to see such timbered architecture, which is as unique to Arecibo as the southwestern townhouse style is to San Germán. In a somewhat different vein, the **Iglesia San Felipe**, between Calles José de Diego and González Marín, boasts an unusual cupola and an anti-nuclear, anti-torture mural.

The **Alcaldía** town hall, tucked at the intersection of Calles José de Diego, Romero Barceló and Juarregui, is among the prettier offices in Puerto Rico, and its inhabitants are among the friendliest and most receptive. A trip there will garner for you information galore – their pamphlet, *Historia de Arecibo Como Capital de Ron*, is a big favorite among rummies and hangers-on – and perhaps a cup of coffee.

Formerly the Plaza Mayor, now the **Plaza Luis Muñoz Rivera**, this must be the prettiest plaza in Puerto Rico, with the cathedral facing over an idiosyncratically landscaped park surrounded by wrought-iron railings and multi-

Left, cheerful resident. **Right**, rum distillery, Arecibo.

colored Spanish colonial architecture. The plaza has undergone an astounding number of transformations in the past 100 years. In the mid-1890s, it was burnt to ashes during a fire that consumed much of the city. In 1899, a hurricane and the ensuing surf, which was not far short of a tidal wave, pounded it into disrepair.

Arecibo was one of the first of the Puerto Rican cities to jump off the Spanish imperial bandwagon and to honor its own native heroes. The monument in memory of Queen Isabella II of Spain, which for so long stood in the middle of the plaza, was replaced in 1927 with an obelisk honoring local hero and politician Luis Muñoz Marín. It's the centerpiece of the town and one of its most scenic features.

Notwithstanding its history of natural disasters, about the only bad thing one can say about the layout of the town is that the river, the Rio Grande de Arecibo, is a volatile creature, and the town does flood with alarming frequency. This, however, only enhances its prestige as an attractive shopping town; regular floods mean regular flood sales of damaged goods.

Star attraction: Anyone who has ever taken sixth-grade or first-form science should have some familiarity with Arecibo. On one of those big, full-page spreads that fill up space in astronomy textbooks, the **Arecibo Observatory** is generally featured prominently.

A complicated trip 20 miles south of the town of Arecibo into the karst country will bring you to the mammoth complex. From downtown Arecibo, follow de Diego to Route 129. Bear left on Route 651 and follow it for the 4 miles before it becomes 635. Travel about the same distance until you come to a T-intersection, at which you'll turn right (onto Route 626) and travel a few hundred yards before making a left on 625, at the end of which is the renowned observatory.

For further details of this, one of the most important research observatories in the Americas, see the panel on the facing page. **Arecibo.**

178

ARECIBO OBSERVATORY

Hidden among the mountains of north-western Puerto Rico, where the stars shine undimmed by city lights, sits the most sensitive radio telescope on Earth.

The Arecibo Ionospheric Observatory is so huge that you can spot it from a jumbo jet at 33,000 ft. Yet on the ground, first-time visitors need a detailed road map to find its guarded entrance.

Located at the end of winding Route 625, in the heart of Puerto Rico's karst country, the observatory has been the focus of numerous astronomical breakthroughs over the years, ranging from Alexander Wolszcan's 1992 discovery of planets outside our own solar system to NASA's recent $100 million Search for Extra-Terrestrial Intelligence.

In 1993, the Arecibo "dish" gained world prominence when two American astronomers, Russell H. Hulse and Joseph H. Taylor, Jr, won the Nobel Prize in Physics for work done using the Arecibo facility.

The Observatory owes its existence largely to Puerto Rico's political status as a United States Commonwealth and to the island's geographic position 17° north of the Equator. That makes it ideal for observation of planets, quasars, pulsars and other cosmic phenomena. The telescope is so sensitive it can detect objects 13 billion light-years away, just by systematically probing the depths of the universe with radio transmitters set at specific wavelengths and listening for their echoes.

Built in 1960, the Arecibo Observatory is funded by an annual $7.5 million grant from the National Science Foundation, though its day-to-day affairs are managed by Cornell University of Ithaca, New York. The observatory counts 130 full-time employees among its staff, and has hosted more than 200 visiting scientists from countries as diverse as Argentina, Bulgaria, Brazil and Russia. No military experiments of any kind are conducted here and, despite the presence of security guards, there's nothing secretive about this place.

The "dish" itself, suspended over a huge natural sinkhole, is by far the largest of its kind in the world. Spanning 1,000 ft in diameter, it covers 20 acres and is composed of nearly 40,000 perforated aluminum mesh panels, each measuring 3 ft by 6 ft. A 600-ton platform is suspended 425 ft over the dish by 12 cables strung from three reinforced concrete towers. In mid-1993, a steel rim was added around the edge of the telescope to block out radio interference from local sources.

Underneath the dish lies a jungle of ferns, orchids and begonias. In fact, tourists can get only as far as a viewing platform high above the site. The dish itself is off-limits, and visitors are presently limited to a five minute audio tape describing the facility and a display area that explains the telescope's construction together with some current scientific results.

However Cornell University is building a $2 million visitors' center, which will include a 120-seat auditorium, a 4,000-sq. ft scientific museum with explanations in English and Spanish, a gift shop and a trail leading to a viewing platform, from which the telescope can be seen at close range.

About 50,000 tourists visit the Arecibo Observatory every year, a number expected to double with the opening of the visitor's center in late 1995. ∎

The dish is hidden in a natural sinkhole.

179

THE KARST COUNTRY

Puerto Rico is one of those places blessed to an almost unfair extent with an enormous variety of beauty of landscape. But such places are legion, and what do you give in Puerto Rico to the tourist who has everything? The answer is not hard to find: the dark green sector of the island's northwest where the land rises in regular green-and-white hillocks and appears to be boiling – the intriguing area known as the karst country.

Limestone sink holes: Karst is one of the world's oddest rock formations and can occur only under the most fortuitous circumstances. Some geologists claim there are only two places on earth where rock formations resemble those of the northwest of the island: one, just across the Mona Passage in the Dominican Republic and one in Yugoslavia.

Karst is formed when water sinks into limestone and erodes larger and larger basins, known as "sinkholes." Many erosions create many sinkholes, until one is left with peaks of land only where the land has not sunk with the erosion of limestone: these are *mogotes*, or karstic hillocks, which resemble each other in size and shape to a striking extent, given the randomness of the process that created them. All this leads you to realize that the highest point on the highest *mogote* in the karst country is certainly below the level the limestone ground held in earlier days when the first drop of rain opened the first sinkhole.

It's hard to say where the karst country begins. Some say at Manatí, though there are two hills not 10 minutes drive west of San Juan which look suspiciously karstic. From Manatí, they carry on as far west as Isabela, and are at their most spectacular a short drive (5 miles) south of the major cities of Puerto Rico's northwest.

It's just as hard to say wherein their appeal lies. Part of it must be in the odd symmetry of the things – despite the fact that it is the holes, not the hills, which

Left, karst formations near Arecibo.

have undergone the change over eons.

These hills are impressive mountains only a hundred feet high – they are probably the grandest landscape within which humans can feel a sense of scale. They encompass a startling variety within their regularity; certain *mogotes* can look like the Arizona desert tucked in for bed in the Black Forest.

The karstic forests: The Department of Natural Resources has recognized the beauty and fragility of this unique karstic landscape. It has created four national forests in which it is protected: **Cambalache, Guajataca, Río Abajo** and **Vega**. Not all the karst country is limited to these forests; in fact, they are woefully small, comprising only about 4,000 acres in total, with Río Abajo accounting for over half of these.

All are ripe for hiking, yet the trails in the karst country never seem as crowded as those up El Yunque and other Puerto Rican mountains. This is due perhaps to the fact that the northwest is still the most isolated part of Puerto Rico, but perhaps is also due to the dangers involved with this sort of landscape. Sinkholes are not like potholes, but they can come as unexpectedly, especially in heavy brush. Get a trail map from the visitors' center at whatever reserve you try. Otherwise, *The Other Puerto Rico*, by Kathryn Robinson, offers helpful advice, and one read of it will convince you that there's nowhere in Puerto Rico that is not worth risking your life to see.

Cars to karst: One of the great pleasures of the karst country is that it is located in the idyllic Puerto Rican northwest, full of prosperous towns, cheerful bars and decent roads. Driving is easy in the karst country, with none of the coronary anxiety most tourists experience in the Cordillera Central.

Arecibo is the capital of the karst country, and some fine drives can begin from there. The easiest is certainly Route 10 south to **Embalse dos Bocas**. Taking 129 southwest to Lares is a pleasant jaunt flanked by *colmados* (grocery stores), which never lets you stray into the Cordillera, as the Route 10 trip is prone to do. If you like karst a lot, though, head west on Route 2, turn left on Route 119, and follow the road to **Lake Guajataca** for the finest views of the water and limestone that made the whole unfathomable but evocative landscape possible.

Make it a point, if at all possible, to get out to the karst country. The unique beauty is staggering, and is worth a visit by itself. Even more, though, the sight of karst will add another dimension to this tropical paradise too often labeled as a place for a "beach vacation."

Frontier town: If this tiny island has a frontier town, surely **Lares** is it. It sits at the western edge of the Cordillera Central's main cluster of peaks, and rests at the southernmost spur of the karst country. Lares is about as far from the sea as one can get in Puerto Rico, and to its west stretches a placid corridor of plains land running just north of the hills of La Cadena and just south of Route 111 and the sleepy Río Culebrinas.

Like many of the towns in this area where plains meet uplands to produce eerily spectacular vistas, Lares is as scenic to approach as it is to leave.

Lake Dos Bocas, near Arecibo.

182

Arriving from the south on either Route 124 or Route 128, the traveler is greeted by a tiny, toylike and close-packed community perched on a gentle rise across a valley and shadowed by rugged twin karstic *mogotes*. Emerging from the east on Route 111 from the karstic clusters of the Río Abajo Forest Reserve, you are hit by surprise at Lares' anomalous urbanity.

The town itself exudes much of the toylike ambience which you may well have perceived from afar. It's an attenuated cluster of little businesses, bars and shops snaking along two main one-way streets that run in opposite directions. In the center of the town is an imposing 19th-century Spanish colonial church, whose pale pastel facade and gracefully arched roof give it something of a Middle Eastern look.

If Lares has a stern side, pride rather than inhospitability is its source. For as the scene of the *Grito de Lares*, Puerto Rico's glorious and ill-fated revolt against Spanish colonial rule, the town is generally considered to be the birthplace of modern Puerto Rican political consciousness.

The Grito de Lares: The *Grito de Lares* ("Shout of Lares") was not merely a Puerto Rican historical event; its roots lay in political grievances that were to sweep Spain's Caribbean colonies in the mid-19th century and result, some decades later, in their ultimate loss.

When, in 1867, native Puerto Rican guards demonstrated in protest at discrepancies between their own salaries and those of Spanish guards, many liberals were expelled from the island, including Ramón Emeterio Betances, a distinguished physician and certainly the most prominent voice in Puerto Rican politics at the time. Betances went to New York, Santo Domingo and Saint Thomas, where he rallied support for abolition and self-determination and met Manuel Rojas, a Venezuelan farmer who lived in Lares. With Rojas, he planned an agrarian revolt in the area.

On September 23, 1868, hundreds of Betances' followers seized Lares and began to march on nearby San Sebastián.

Clara Cave, in the Camuy complex.

There they were met by Spanish forces, and easily routed. Though Betances was merely exiled to France and the revolution came to nought, the *Grito de Lares* led Puerto Ricans to think differently of their land and their aspirations for it, and the spirit of that September day lives on not only in the streets of Lares, but in the hearts and on the tongues of Puerto Ricans throughout the island.

Speleology and scatology: Also significant, but in a rather different way, is the unspectacular town of **Camuy**, just far enough west of Arecibo, just far enough north of Route 2, to appear almost untouched by the life of modern Puerto Rico. What appeal Camuy has is more primordial – a bewildering maze of one-way streets that will never accommodate automobiles; a lifestyle tranquil to the point of torpor; a few vestiges of an older era, like shops that sell salves and incense for the appeasement of various saints; and, most primordial of all, one of the largest cave systems in the western world.

Most easily reachable by driving due south on Route 129, the cave system is actually a series of karstic sinkholes connected by the 350-foot-deep Camuy River, which burrows underground through soft limestone for much of its course from the Cordillera to the Atlantic. The largest of these entrances has been developed for tourism, with attractions of the "fun for the whole family" variety.

The **Río Camuy Cave Park**, which is managed by the Puerto Rico Land Administration, contains one of the most massive cave networks in the Western Hemisphere. This 268-acre complex includes three crater-like sinkholes and one cave. The Taínos considered these formations sacred; their artifacts have been found throughout the area. The park's main attraction is 170-foot high Clara Cave, which is specially lit, accessible only by trolley and only in guided groups.

The cave entrance looks like a cathedral facade, with a broad row of toothy stalactites descending from the bushy hillside. Inside the cave's overhang, the light becomes bluish, and a weird silence descends, broken only by the chirp of bats on the ceiling and minute distant echoes. Could it be the far-off sound of water dripping through yet undiscovered passages?

It could be, but it's not. It's bat droppings, and you won't have to travel more than a dozen steps to realize that much of it is very likely to fall on you in the course of your perambulations. Natives claim that the droppings are potentially extremely toxic. But don't let this keep you away. Wash afterwards, or cover up well but visit. There's nothing quite like it.

Leaving the cave park, you have two excellent choices for lunch not far away. The **Restaurante Las Cavernas** and the **Restaurante El Taíno**, both located along Route 129, pride themselves on traditional Puerto Rican cuisine, bilingual waiters, family atmosphere and fairly reasonable prices. At Las Cavernas, the house specialty is *arroz con guinea* (rice with hen), served on a large plate with beans and *amarillos* (fried bananas) for dessert.

Right, window on the world. Below, keeping watch.

SAN SEBASTIÁN AND THE COAST TOWNS

Of all the prosperous and provincial towns of Puerto Rico's northwest, **San Sebastián** stands out as the most representative of the region and in the most noticeable contrast to the gloomy villages of the Cordillera Central which lie to the south and east.

Perhaps this is because it is the first of the towns which is truly out of the highlands and secure in its footing as part of the low-lying northwest. Perhaps too it has something to do with the cornucopia of food products the region produces, for this is the heart of many of the island's oldest and most traditional food industries.

San Sebastián is surrounded by green and moist rolling grassland, and stood as one of Puerto Rico's sugar boom towns in the cane industry's heyday. Now, the area is given over to scattered dairy farming and various agricultural pursuits which used to be associated with other parts of the island. Tobacco grows in many a valley, and coffee plants, once the preserve of Yauco and other towns in the island's arid southwest, can be seen growing on many a local hillside.

With close to 40,000 residents, most of them living in the shady main streets that cluster about a lovely plaza, San Sebastián has more of an urban ambience than most of the northwest. It lacks the historical reputation of Lares and as a commercial center is utterly overwhelmed by the tuna fishing port of Mayagüez which is just 10 miles away on the east coast.

But San Sebastián is within easy driving distance of these places and has a number of charming features that they lack: it is the most provincial of moderate-sized Puerto Rican cities with a thriving local culture and most of the modern amenities; big salsa groups like El Gran Combo de Puerto Rico play here, as do first-run films.

This is not to say San Sebastián is devoid of scenic charms either. There's no better spot from which to explore the wondrous karst country. There's also the famous Pozo del Virgen, a well that is a religious shrine which attracts thousands of devout Catholics every year. To the north, **Lake Guajataca** boasts nature walks and a *parador* hotel, as well as excellent fishing. And any drive into the countryside will invariably lead to scenic surprises.

Surprising town: The most amazing story Puerto Ricans tell about the town of **Quebradillas** concerns basketball. During a close regular season game between the Quebradillas team and archrival Isabela, the score became close, and tensions and tempers began to run high. When Isabela took the lead on a surprise basket and its supporters began to cheer and taunt, Quebradillas's town dignitary, Mayor Hernández rose from the stands with a revolver and fired into the opposing stands, injuring several spectators.

This is not to point to the people of Quebradillas as being especially violent – if anything, their friendly and welcoming attitude will convince you the

opposite is the case – but rather to show that in this isolated northwestern municipality, anything can happen, and quite often anything does. Quebradillas itself adds to the appealing oddities you expect from the towns west of Arecibo – spiritualist herb shops, narrow streets and houses sloping towards the waterline – with some geological oddities that make it a town well worth going out of your way for.

A short drive or walk northwest of town, **Playa Guajataca**, described paradoxically by locals as a "nice, dangerous beach," is to be taken with caution. Deep waters, white sands and raging surf make it highly attractive for surfers and bathers, but highly dangerous for those incapable of swimming the English Channel. Even experts should exercise caution.

The **Río Guajataca** is another spot as beautiful as it is forbidding, and pocked with a cave system which, though not completely charted, appears to be as extensive and awesome as that of the caves at Camuy.

Nearby **Lake Guajataca**, 7 miles south on Route 113, is man-made, as are the rest of Puerto Rico's lakes, but offers a splendid natural retreat, with two *paradores*, Vistamar and Guajataca, both situated on the coast, serving as convenient bases for hikes into the rolling **Aymamon Mountains** in the **Guajataca Forest Reserve**, which are located just to the west.

Isabela, the next town along the coast, is a florilegium of all the charms of Puerto Rico's northwestern corner, with a cluster of brilliant, whitewashed houses tumbling out of the hills to some of the island's most justly renowned surfing and swimming beaches.

The city has that look of stability and purposefulness which is so characteristic of the region, due perhaps to flourishing shoe and textile industries. But Isabela has not bought serenity at the price of industrial over-expansion; it has retained a high proportion of its small farms.

If history has been somewhat kind to Isabela, nature has not. Located just

Plaza, San Sebastían.

south of the tectonically fickle Milwaukee Trench, Isabela has been victimized by earthquakes and tidal waves for as long as it has been settled.

The most memorable of the quakes – on October 11, 1918 – destroyed much of the town, including the renowned **Iglesia de San Antonio de Padua**. The reconstructed church on Calle Celso Barbosa, which was built in 1924, is worth a visit; the subtle facade and delicate double cupolas recreate aspects of the original design.

Horse enthusiasts should make their way to **Arenales**, to the south, where a number of the fine *pasofino* stables have made Isabela a renowned equine breeding center.

Most visitors to Isabela, however, come to ride waves, not steeds, and **Jobos Beach**, just west of town on Route 466, is the place to do that.

The beach is made even more beautiful by the high cliffs which back it. One of these, **El Pozo de Jacinto**, is the source of a charming – though rather sad – local custom. A farmer named Jacinto used to pasture his cows near the edge of the cliffs. One day, part of the cliff collapsed and Jacinto's finest bovine tumbled to her death. Jacinto, enraged, ran to the cliff's edge and cursed fate. Fate disapproved; Jacinto too fell off the cliff and died. Today, Isabela schoolchildren stand at the edge of the cliffs and yell: "*Jacinto! Damne la vaca!*" (Damn the cow!) It's supposed to bring good luck.

Rival resorts: The two lovely seaside towns of **Aguada** and **Aguadilla** on the west coast have a running rivalry over which was the spot where Christopher Columbus first landed in Puerto Rico. As such, its residents might be taken aback to find that most of the handful of visitors who come each year have a hard enough time telling the two towns apart, let alone judging the primacy of their respective claims.

In defence of its claim, **Aguada** has erected a seaside **Parque de Colón** a mile northwest of town on Route 441, dead center of **Playa Espinar**, a 2,500-foot white sand beach so enticing that

Pounding surf at Isabela.

Columbus buffs will wish their man had landed there, regardless of historical fact. Aguadillans, meanwhile, certainly have logic, if not an airtight argument on their side in claiming that Columbus's men stopped for water at the spring which now forms the focus of their own **Parque El Parterre**.

Aguadilla is the more prosperous and picturesque of the two towns, and has more places to stay, including the *parador* El Faro. It's laid out like a Mediterranean resort, bleeding along a mile of coast with very little penetration inland. **Avenida José de Jesús Esteves** (Route 440) is a prim and polychromatic seaside boulevard, a little Caribbean equivalent of the Promenade des Anglais in Nice; parallel streets are punctuated with attractive if unspectacular parks. *Mundillo* lace and wicker hats are the twin prides of Aguadilla's active artisan community and both are ubiquitous in the shops located in the commercial district.

Flyers and playas: Many though its charms may be, Aguadilla can't claim, like Aguada, to have a pleasant *balneario* (swimming area) at its doorstep. Aguadilla's is just a bit too rocky for sane people to have a go at.

Most of the townspeople, therefore, head north on Route 197, to do their bathing at **Playa Boqueron Sur**, known locally as Crash Boat Beach in honor of the vessels which used to take off from there to rescue errant fighter planes from the former **Ramey Air Force Base** just to the north, which has the longest runway in the Caribbean. The Ramey Air Force Base is now no longer in service and the area is being developed for civilian use.

Rincón, southwest of Aguadilla on a point on the way to Mayagüez, is certainly not a place for bathing enthusiasts, except for those whose idea of a good time is being thrown face-first onto rock flats or jagged reefs. Nor, although nightlife here is fast and loose enough for any taste, is it partying that draws so many young people to Rincón from San Juan, which is by now 100 miles away. In fact, what Rincón has

Crossing the Plaza, Aguada.

lures the young and the strong from much further than just San Juan.

International waves: The town has a dazzling and varied offshore surf which has drawn board enthusiasts for decades, and has made Rincón, since the World Surfing Championships were held here in 1968, the surfing capital of the Caribbean area. Also offshore, but a little further out, is a wintering place for hump-back whales, although whale-watching has not yet been developed as a tourist business.

Though *rincón* means "corner," the town actually sits at the flat, regular end of the peninsula shaped like a pointer's snout. This is **La Cadena Hills**, the westernmost spur of the rugged Cordillera Central, and nowhere in Puerto Rico do mountains meet coast more dramatically than they do here. The view most surfers see from offshore is of deep green hills and shimmering groves of mango backing bright, white sand and turquoise sea, and it's highly possible that this unique vista draws as many surfers to Rincón as the sport itself – though they tend to spend more time admiring the views than they do riding the waves.

Tunnel vision: Still, it's hard to imagine better surfing anywhere. Rincón is not just one beach, but six, bordered by picturesque and prominent coral reefs and shoals, stretching from Puerto Rico's rough Atlantic coast on the north side of the peninsula to the placid and eminently swimmable turquoise waters of the Caribbean south. The quality and size of the surf varies all the way along the peninsula, leaving boardmen with a choice of rides at all levels of difficulty. The effect is rather like that of a year-round ski resort with a great number of delightful trails.

The town of Rincón is pleasant and quiet, with a number of trendy, surfer-infested restaurants ranged along Route 115. An old disused nuclear power plant standing next to the town's quaint, little lighthouse lends the area an eerie look and gives Rincón an other-worldliness perceptible even to the non-surfers who end up here by mistake.

Going for a ride in the Aguadillan surf.

THE SOUTH COAST

Until the completion in 1975 of Route 52, the Autopista Luís Ferré, toll road, San Juan natives considered the prospect of driving to Ponce only slightly less daunting than that of swimming to Miami. Indeed, Puerto Rico's south coast used to be so isolated by the Cordillera and its tortuous one-lane roads that a majority of Puerto Ricans saw their southern compatriots in terms of a number of bizarre and often unflattering stereotypes. These were the proud, stubborn farmers, whose accent was slightly odd: they were a simple people with something of a gift for politics but with a culture you wouldn't envy if you lived at the bottom of the ocean. Their only inheritance was a landscape as gorgeous as it was remote.

All that has changed, and it's no longer even possible to entertain those stereotypes. The south has charms that are drawing northerners an hour down the highway to take residence. Ponce, recently much refurbished with a glittering double plaza and the greatest art museum in the Caribbean, is as pleasant and cultured as any city of its size anywhere.

Salinas' seafood restaurants rival San Juan's best, and Jobos Bay is as pleasant a spot for picnicking as it is for sailing. All along the coast is the alluring, typically southern landscape of golden plain stretching between lush mountain and blue Caribbean. And from Ponce, it's now only 90 minutes to get to San Juan. Most *ponceños* would tell you it's not worth the effort.

Preceding page, ~troleum and sugarcane, the two major industries, near Yabucoa; Spa... ~nial house, Guayama. **Left**, Playa las Palmas, Punta la Galiena.

HUMACAO TO JOBOS BAY

Humacao is a first-rate industrial center with pretensions to being a first-rate resort. Some of these pretensions are justified. The city, only a 45-minute drive from San Juan via Route 30, is within 2 miles of some of the most dazzling beachfront Vieques Sound has to offer. Add to that its convenience as a starting point for excursions in the southeast, and Humacao becomes a place that has to be taken seriously as a holiday retreat.

The best way to begin a beach tour of this part of the island is to head north to **Playa Humacao**, probably the best equipped public beach on the island. The beach boasts not only miles of bright sand and a handful of offshore cays, but also a veritable arcade of lockers, refreshment stands and other amenities. The beach benefits from its size, drawing heavily enough from local and tourist groups alike to ensure there's always something going on, if only a pickup volleyball game: join in.

Halfway down the eastern coast and a 10-minute drive south from Humacao is **Palmas del Mar**, Puerto Rico's largest vacation resort. The self-appointed "New American Riviera," this 2,700-acre (1,100-hectare) holiday heaven comprises just about everything but a monorail: 20 tennis courts ("Is there a court available?" "No, sir, not 'til Thursday."), a gorgeous beachfront golf course, riding stables, fine beaches, deep-sea fishing, eight restaurants, numerous bars, an ice cream shop, and so on. Palmas del Mar has proved itself popular both among families and conventioneers.

Monkey business: A little less than a mile off the coast of Playa Humacao lies an anomalous island that few have had the opportunity to visit. This place, **Cayo Santiago**, is home for approximately 700 rhesus monkeys.

With a grant from Columbia University, the animals were brought from India to Puerto Rico in 1938 for research into primate behavior. Never before had such a social troupe of monkeys been transported into the Western world and placed in semi-natural conditions. The comfortable climate and undisturbed environment of Cayo Santiago still left many experts skeptical on the question of whether the primates could survive and breed.

For two years, tuberculosis scourged the colony. Then, during World War II, grant money ran out and the monkeys faced the threat of starvation. Townspeople from nearby Playa de Humacao supported the colony by taking bananas, coconuts and other available foods out to the island several times each week for the duration of the war. (Nowadays the animals tend to feed on commercial monkey food.)

Since 1938, more than 300 scientific articles have been published about the colony. Unfortunately, though, due to possible health hazards (and the fact that rhesus monkeys have large canine teeth and at times can be very aggressive), visitors without credentials are not allowed on the island.

Left, Palmas del Mar golfing. **Right**, bathing at Palmas del Mar.

Cane sugar center: From Humacao to **Yabucoa** (a native Indian term meaning "Place of the Yucca Trees"), rolling hills, semi-tropical forests, sugarcane fields and cow pastures highlight an exceedingly pleasant drive. Just before reaching Yabucoa, Route 3 passes the **Roig Sugar Mill**, a rusty piece of antiquity which is one of the few survivors of the southeast's agricultural economy, which unfortunately has gone belly-up. During the harvest season (January to June), you can see how the stacks of harvested cane get shredded and pressed to extract juices which later become refined sugar.

Yabucoa marks the beginning of an industrial circuit that continues south-westward. Taking advantage of low-wage labor and liberal tax laws, oil refineries, pharmaceutical companies, textile manufacturers and industrial chemical plants border the smaller towns all the way down the coast.

Leaving Yabucoa, Route 901 takes you on a scenic drive southward (part of the Ruta Panoramica) through arid coastal headlands which form part of the Cuchilla de Pandura Mountains.

Ghost beach: A few kilometers away from town along the **Balneario Lucia** shore, abandoned seafood restaurants indicate that, at one point, this spot was believed to have potential as a popular bathing retreat. Now, it's a ghost beach; few bother with it. Rows of planted coconut palm trees grow in awkwardly misshapen directions along the beach. The trunks of these trees are wrapped with sheet metal, apparently to prevent rats from climbing them.

The rats, apparently, have joy-riding in mind. According to a native writer: "When there are no such bands, rats with a penchant for primitive piloting climb the trunks, nibble a hole in the coconuts, lap out the milk, crawl through the hole into the nut, gnaw off the stem and sit inside the shell as it makes its break-neck descent to the ground…"

Route 901 curves upward into a series of hills overlooking rugged shoreline and a Caribbean expanse, with the island of Vieques viewed through a haze in the distance.

Built on an impressive vista point, **El Horizonte**, a touristy-looking restaurant, gives the opportunity to savor reasonably priced local seafood while looking out to sea.

Down to Punta Tuna: The road descends from the hills to **Punta Tuna**, where one of Puerto Rico's active lighthouses rests. Built in the 1890s by Spain, the lighthouse is now run by the US Coast Guard. Adjacent to Punta Tuna, a little-known beach ranks among the nicest on the southeastern coast.

Farther down the road, on the opposite side of Punta Tuna, another good beach arches more than a kilometer around tiny **Puerto Maunabo**. Pack a lunch in the morning before setting out from Yabucoa. A lunch break on one of these lovely beaches is the perfect interlude on this circular trip.

The Ruta Panoramica continues past the town of Maunabo and winds up a narrow road past cliffside houses and damp verdure over the Cuchilla de Pandura and back to Yabucoa.

Unspoilt corner: You can tell you're in

Left, Punta Tuna. Below, playing dominoes at Maunabo.

the southeastern corner of Puerto Rico when the local residents stop having marketing preconceptions about their part of the island. This place is not karstic or dry or cosmopolitan. Nonetheless, it's Puerto Rican landscape at its least spoiled.

Guayama and **Aguirre** hold little in common besides the fact that both border on **Jobos Bay**, one of the finest protected shallow-water areas on the island. Ichthyologists (fish enthusiasts) and ornithologists will love the area several species of Puerto Rican birds unseen elsewhere on the island frequent the place, and fish are well-served by the bay's healthy quantity of microorganisms.

The fishing is good everywhere, but legal only outside of protected waters. This means you need a boat, but boating is a very popular pastime in Jobos Bay, and *ponceños* frequently include the area in daytrips that depart from Caja de Muertos.

Arroyo, with what some consider its sister city Patillas, is one of the most

down-to-earth of Puerto Rican towns. The landscape surrounding the city is fetching, if unspectacular – it's a reedy, bushy sort of place. The beaches by both towns are uncrowded and pleasant, and weather generally makes beaching even more secure a prospect than it is in the immediate neighborhood of San Juan. The **Embalse de Patillas**, a short drive up Route 184 from that city, makes a fine place for a lakeside picnic on the way into the Cordillera.

Salinas is one of the most enjoyable and undersung towns on this island. It has more of a southwestern ethos than most of the urbanizations surrounding it. There are several possible reasons for this: one could be that it maintains a shade of cosmopolitanism of the sort practised in Ponce and Mayagüez, which have expatriate populations. Another is that perhaps its many excellent seafood restaurants serve up redfish, lobster and other *criollo* specials of a quality that puts the Mona Passage – the stretch of water between Puerto Rico and the Dominican Republic – in one's mind.

Eastern allure: Despite its western orientation, most of Salinas' allure lies to the east. Its downtown is an attractive one, but after a brief stop you may want to get on the road to Aguirre to visit one of the most lively and patronized *galleras* on the island.

A *gallera* is a ring for cock-fighting, a sport many people find distasteful. But if you want to stay for the experience you will see men knowledgeable about fighting cocks wager hundreds of dollars on the local birds. Be careful though. The sport is bloody and hardly for the fainthearted, and there will be plenty of people willing to take your wagers. (And be aware there aren't any odds posted.)

Not too far away, **Punta Salinas** offers a slew of unpretentious seafood restaurants, several of which look out on the peaceful **Bahia de Rincón**, and all of which serve seafood the likes of which would cause the most finicky chef in all of San Juan to turn green with envy, and perhaps even tempt some of the east coast's most scrupulous fishermen to order another plate.

Activities in Guayama. **Left**, taking the sun and **Right**, strolling.

PONCE AND SURROUNDINGS

No one ever claimed that Puerto Ricans were not a proud people, but it still shocks even *sanjuaneros* to hear a Ponceño refer to this birthplace as "La Perla del Sur," or "The Pearl of the South." It's to be expected that tourism companies and travel agencies will exploit such a sobriquet, but should the natives themselves be waxing lyrical – remembering that there are close to 200,000 of them?

Perhaps most surprising is the fact that **Ponce**, Puerto Rico's second-largest city, actually is a pearl of sorts. Though not so distant in the imagination of travelers as Mayagüez, it's still far enough away from the San Juan/Cerromar/Palmas del Mar circuit most travelers cling to. But now Ponce is an easy 90-minute drive from San Juan on the Autopista Luís Ferré, and there's very little excuse for not heading south to see what all these southerners are

Preceding pages: Ponce's celebrated Parque de Bombas. **Left**, Ponce Cathedral.

bragging about. On an island where self-congratulation is a way of life, the people of Ponce have the reputation of being almost haughty. And anyone outside deepest San Juan will admit that *ponceños* have a right to be aloof.

Hot stuff: To begin with, Ponce has the best weather on the island. It's located in what ecologists call a "rain shadow;" the afternoon storms which beleaguer the north coast are stopped dead by the peaks of the Cordillera Central. You can see the rain from Ponce – it's in those purple clouds pulsing about the hills 10 miles north – but you're not going to feel any of it.

The landscape surrounding the city shows the same typical southwestern pastiche of purple and lavender skies against tumbling grasslands, parched to gold by the Caribbean sun. This is not the Atlantic – although a place as far south as Puerto Rico can take on its hostile cobalt aspect – as a look south from the hills above town will demonstrate. Especially from El Vígia Hill, the view across Ponce shows the coral and white of the town's stately houses, the turquoise waters of its Caribbean harbor and the stripes of green mangrove and travertine coral formations of the archipelago surrounding the big isle of Caja de Muertos.

This is not the impression you'll get as you enter the town on Route 2, the antiquated proto-expressway. Here, your first sight of Ponce is of the Ponce bypass, which links highways 52 and 2, traveling through a neighborhood of unmitigated tedium. This is where the shopping malls, the roadside fruit stands and the gas stations are.

The inland port: But Ponce proper – and if there's a proper city in Puerto Rico, it's Ponce – is not as far away as one might expect. This is perhaps the archetype of a strangely Puerto Rican sort of city; a bustling port with an enviable natural harbor which has nonetheless developed around a city center some distance inland. A left turn will take you, not to the center of a bustling waterfront town, but to the interesting outpost at **Playa de Ponce** and the wharf at **Muelle de Ponce**. To get into the heart

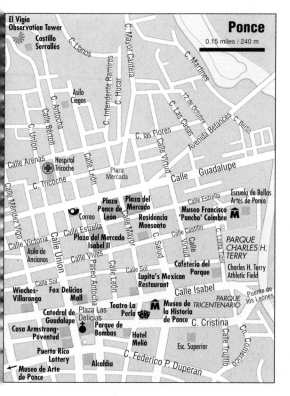

of Ponce, continue in a northwesterly direction on Route 133 as it passes over the sluggish Río Portugues and becomes **Calle F. P. Duperan**, the main commercial street of the town, also known as Calle Comercio.

Here, you'll see the results of the $450 million "Ponce en Marcha" program, begun in 1986 by former Governor Rafael Hernández Colón, himself a *ponceño*. The massive beautification effort resulted in the burying of unsightly phone and electric cables, the repaving of streets and the renovation of nearly every structure which is located in the downtown district. Hernández Colón is no longer governor, and the program has recently run out of money, but its astounding success was enough to turn Ponce into one of the Caribbean's most beautiful cities. Its image was further boosted in 1993 when Ponce hosted the 17th Central American and Caribbean Games.

A square deal: At the end of Calle Duperan is the cluster of architectural beauties which gives Ponce its reputa-tion as one of the most Spanish of Puerto Rican cities. Here the magnificent **Plaza Central**, lush and beautifully landscaped, sits pounded by sunlight amidst a pinwheel of centuries-old streets. It's actually a double plaza, with **Plaza Degetau** and **Plaza Muñoz Rivera** sitting kitty-cornered across Calle Cristina. Both are similarly landscaped, with huge fig-trees in lozenge-shaped topiary and large, shady islands of grass. Broad paths of rose-colored granite weave through the parks; they're lined with slender old lamp-posts which make the plaza both attractive and accessible in the evening.

Plaza Degetau is dominated by the **Cathedral of Our Lady of Guadeloupe**, named for the patron saint of Ponce. It's a pretty, low, pinkish structure, reminiscent in its colors and rounded turrets of San Juan Cathedral. Though not as old as San Juan's, having been begun in the late 17th century, Ponce's cathedral makes ample use of the flood of reflected sunlight from the plaza. Its silvery towers – a characteris- **Plaza del Mercado.**

tically Puerto Rican touch in religious architecture – are shaped like little hydrants, and glow oddly at midday. This gives the cathedral a bright, inviting look, against which the eerie stillness of its interior is a shocking contrast.

Photo opportunity: Our Lady of Guadelupe may hold the religious high ground, but the building right behind it cuts more ice with the tourist crowd. This is the **Parque de Bombas**, Ponce's Victorian firehouse, and it's surely the oddest building on an island that has never been shy of architectural improvisation. With its red and black walls and playful collection of poles, sideboards, crenellations and cornices, it's a gaudy and riotous building with a playful, truly *ponceño* spirit. It's also the most photographed building in Puerto Rico. The **Alcaldía**, diagonally across the plaza from the two buildings, has a pleasant hacienda feeling to it and contrasts in a lively way with its two more renowned neighbors.

Around town: There are plenty of peaceful perambulations to be made in this most historic part of Ponce. **Calle Cristina** and **Calle Mayor** are particularly renowned for the wrought-iron grill and balcony work which evoke in Ponce, as in San Juan, the spirit of European cities. Even the highly commercialized Calle Duperan boasts a number of quaint shops and a shady marketplace. The finest market in town, however, is in the **Plaza del Mercado**, which is located two blocks north of the Plaza Central on Calle Atocha between Calles Estrella and Castillo. Here, merchants haggle with customers over anything that can be worn, ogled or eaten, in an ambience as charged with excitement as any market in San Juan.

Definitely worth visiting is the **Museo de la Historia de Ponce**, which was inaugurated December 12, 1992 – Ponce's 300th anniversary – and is considered Puerto Rico's best civic museum. Two hours in this place, and you'll emerge an expert on all aspects of Ponce's history: geographic, economic, political, racial, medical, educational and industrial. The museum is housed

PONCE ART MUSEUM

In addition to having one of the Caribbean's most beautifully renovated downtown districts, Ponce also prides itself on the region's best art museum: The Museo de Arte de Ponce.

Governor Luís A. Ferré, a *ponceño* and founder of the pro-statehood New Progressive Party, dreamed up the museum in the late 1950s. The institution was born in 1959, and seven years later moved into its present home – a long, low-slung modern building designed by American architect Edward Durrell Stone. It is located along busy Avenida Las Américas, across the street from Catholic University and down the road from another Ponce landmark, a gnarled, 550-year-old *ceiba* tree.

Ferré, now in his nineties, started the Ponce Art Museum off with 71 paintings; today it possesses more than 1,800 registered works, many of them European masterpieces. A marble plaque at the entrance states the museum's purpose: "To broaden the understanding of our own and other

cultures through the contact with and appreciation of the visual arts, thus to enhance the quality of life in Puerto Rico."

Inside, the museum is a honeycomb of skylit hexagonal rooms. Its interior highlight is perhaps its modernistic, scallop-shaped, wooden central staircase, which leads to a cluster of Renaissance paintings.

To appreciate the museum fully, try to visit its galleries in chronological order. The best way is to start in the lobby surrounding the unusual staircase. Here are the oldest paintings in the collection, 14th-century works such as *Madonna and Child* by Luca di Tommé, *A Hebrew Prophet* by Giovanni del Biondo, and Leandro Rosanno's 16th-century masterpiece, *The Flood*.

Upstairs, in the Spanish School gallery, are masterpieces like Alonso Sánchez Coello's *Lady With a Pink*, and two works by José de Ribera, *St. Paul* and *St. Jerome*, as well as Pedro de Mena's lifelike sculpture, *Sorrowing Virgin*. In the adjacent Flemish School can be found Peter Paul Rubens' *The Greek Magus* and David Teniers' *The Temptation of St. Anthony*.

Three adjoining galleries are dedicated to Italian art alone. They are the Northern Italian School (Giovanni Battista Langetti's *The Torture of Ixion*), the Florence and Bologna Schools (Ludovico Cigola's *St. Francis of Assisi*) and the Rome and Naples Schools (*Antiochus and Stratonice* by Pompeo Girolamo Batoni).

The Dutch School gallery contains both Peter Verelst's *The Philosopher* and the *Vanitas* still life of 1678 by Pieter Roestraeten. The last gallery on the second floor is the French School, containing among other works, *The Origin of Painting* by Louis-Jean-François Cagrene, and *Greek Lady at the Bath* by Joseph Marie Vien.

Downstairs, behind glass in the British School gallery, is Sir Frederick Leighton's *Flaming June*, completed in 1895, the year before his death. This painting has become a symbol of the museum itself. Above it hangs *Sleeping Beauty* by Sir Edward Burne-Jones, and on the entire far wall, Burne-Jones' masterpiece, *The Sleep of King Arthur in Avalon* – one of the largest works in the entire collection.

There's enough here for a whole day; few places in Puerto Rico are more worth visiting than the Ponce Art Museum.

A surprise in every room.

THE SOUTHWEST

The part of Puerto Rico furthest from San Juan is, not surprisingly, the part most tourists would choose to visit had they an inkling of what awaits them there. This is Puerto Rico at its best and, in many ways, at its most typical: maritime, mountainous and metropolitan. Mayagüez sits at the center of the region, a city with a vibrancy and beauty which has led Puerto Ricans to ruminate, despite Ponce's recent rehabilitation, "What's Puerto Rico's second city, Ponce or Mayagüez?"

None of the surrounding area, however, will make one sorry one left Mayagüez; there is San Germán, home to several rare examples of Gothic architecture and Puerto Rico's second oldest city; Boquerón, surf capital of the southwest; Parguera, with a phosphorescent bay many consider the best in the world; Guánica, where, for better or for worse, the US Marines were to stage an invasion in 1898 which was to transform Puerto Rico forever; Punta Jagüey, which boasts not only spectacular beaches, but also one of the most beautiful lighthouses in the Atlantic Ocean.

All right, you're lazy and having a helluva time in San Juan. Tear yourself away and go to the southwest. Don't worry. It's civilized there; they have *piña coladas*.

GUAYANILLA AND GUÁNICA

Though the charms of the rippling, brown-green, semi-arid landscapes of Puerto Rico's southwest are well-known to those who love the island, few travelers take the effort to visit some of its charming cities. Nonetheless, the scenic, historic and hedonistic pleasures **Guayanilla** and **Guánica** offer are enough to repay a visit of several days.

Route 2 moves swiftly westwards out of Ponce, and within minutes is running along one of its most inspiring stretches, where it hugs the shore for about 2 miles. Where Route 2 meets the coast it meets one of Greater Ponce's most popular beaches.

Playa El Tuque, 3 miles outside the city, is one of the tinier swimmable beaches on the island. It lies on the western shore of a tiny node of land, most of which is occupied by the marshy lands surrounding the **Laguna de las Salinas** 5 miles outside Ponce. From certain points are good views of Ponce and its bay, and the views to sea include turquoise waters and isolated coral islands. The beach you'll pass just to the left of the highway is known as **Balneario Las Cucharas** ("Spoons Bathing Area"), and the name is apt: it appears to have been gently scooped into a crescent by the calm waters.

Ports and pretty towns: From Las Cucharas, Route 2 runs the pretty 6 miles into Guayanilla. This is a pretty town with a very southwestern flavor. It lies a little over a mile inland, though, and is somewhat quiet. The real attractions of Guayanilla are to the south.

A mile away, at the mouth of the Río Guayanilla, is the desolate and hushed fishing port at **Playa de Guayanilla**. The bay itself is an amazing natural formation: 3 miles wide and embraced by two large peninsulas – **Punta Gotay** and **Punta Verraco** – it is surely one of the most auspiciously formed natural harbors in the Caribbean. A number of peninsulas within the harbor give it at least five sheltered sub-inlets.

The Isle of Java: That's hardly the last you'll hear of Guayanilla Bay – the landscape that surrounds it is full of some of the lushest protected semi-arid forest in the world, and crowded with reminders of a signal episode in both Puerto Rican and American history; an American naval landing described on the following page. But not to make a circuit of the area is to miss the forest for the trees.

The charming town of **Yauco** lies 3 miles west of Guayanilla on Routes 2 and 127. The latter is probably the more pleasant route, except when it rains, which on this arid coast is about once every millennium. Anyone with the most cursory experience of driving in the southwest knows that those little oily bushes huddled on the brown hillsides are coffee trees, but few know the pre-eminence that the Yauco area holds as a coffee capital. By the late 19th century, Puerto Rico had developed the most advanced coffee industry in the world. In the coffeehouses of late-colonial Europe – in Vienna, London, Paris, and Madrid – Puerto Rican coffee was con-

Left, Casa Gordo Beach, Guánica. **Below**, in Patillas.

sidered the very best that one could drink. "Yauco" was that coffee's name.

For whatever can be said about its other effects, the 20th-century presence of Americans on the island removed Yauco from this position of pre-eminence, as emphasis on manufacturing and cane production sapped the industry's resources. Fortunately, vestiges of that halcyon era remain – the stately homes of Yauco's coffee barons.

Owing to the variety of sub-climates in the southwest, coffee was a mobile industry, and its scions and their residences were no less itinerant than their crops. Thus, Yauco shares with San Germán and Mayagüez an architecture that is distinctively Puerto Rican and among the best Spanish-influenced work of its day. Some of these old residences are open to the public; for information on the southwestern style and how to see it, the best source is the **Colegio de Arquitectos**, located in the Casa Rosa, not far from El Morro in Old San Juan.

Even more fortunate is the fact that Yauco has regained some of its old prominence as a coffee-producer and exporter. One of Puerto Rico's most successful brands, Yauco Selecto, is now sold in Japanese gourmet coffee shops for over $20 a pound.

Warships by woodlands: On to Guánica, 5½ miles past Yauco on Route 116. About the same size as Guayanilla, but with an understandably more oceanic ambience, Guánica might be worth visiting even without the historic significance which draws so many travelers and historians. In the mid-summer of 1898, at the height of the Spanish American War, General Nelson Miles, having had no success in a month-long attempt to break Spanish defenses around San Juan, landed in Guánica with a detachment of troops before going on to Ponce. He had come, he said, "to bring you protection, not only to yourselves but to your property, to promote your prosperity, and to bestow upon you the immunities and blessings of the liberal institutions of our government."

Out of this promise came American Puerto Rico, and the degree to which the promise has been kept or breached has circumscribed almost all political arguments on the island for the past 100 years. Predictably, the American arrival is often referred to as an invasion – the commemorative stone placed at the edge of Guánica Harbor by the Puerto Rican chapter of the Daughters of The American Revolution certainly takes that line.

The birds: Though they weren't arriving for the bird-watching, the American forces who landed at Guánica chose as their target the ornithological capital of Puerto Rico. Covering 1,570 acres of subtropical dry forest, the **Guánica Forest Reserve** is home to half of Puerto Rico's bird species. Most treasured among these is the highly endangered Puerto Rican whippoorwill, but if you don't see one, there are plenty of other birds to satisfy your curiosity. This low-lying area also houses 48 of the island's endangered plant species, 16 of which are endemic to the forest. Well-kept hiking trails and a pleasant if unspectacular beach make the forest reserve a deserving spot for a leisurely respite in a hectic schedule of sightseeing.

Below, oyster stand, **Boquerón**. **Right**, Lake **Yauco**.

SAN GERMÁN

Seeds of colonization in the New World have not always brought culture, but they have generally brought overpopulation, and the capitals of the Americas, with their millions of citizens, were generally in place, if only as minor outposts, a couple of centuries ago. **San Germán**, with its population of 30,000, is a different sort of locale – it is one of those major towns of the 16th century which has been blessed by never having been too thoroughly dragged into the squalid rat race of the modern world. Although old, it has never grown into a sprawling urban center. Inch-for-inch, it is the most historic town in all Puerto Rico, perhaps in all the Caribbean.

San Germán is a diamond in an emerald setting, a pearly white town tucked in an uncharacteristically lush and verdant section of the island's south coast about halfway between Ponce and Mayagüez on pretty Route 119.

Although both make claims for their status, neither of these two latter metropolises is Puerto Rico's second city; San Germán is. Founded in 1573 by the second wave of Spanish colonists, it was San Juan's only rival for prominence on the island until the 19th century. Forces invading or retreating from San Juan, notably the English, French and Dutch, not uncommonly stopped in San Germán to arm themselves or lick their wounds. In the 19th century, it became one of Puerto Rico's great coffee towns, with magnates building some of the truly unique homes on the island.

Today, San Germán owes its prominence and cultural vibrancy to the Inter-American University, with its 8,000 students and well-tended grounds, and the diligence with which it has preserved some of the earliest European architectural works to survive in the Western hemisphere.

Heaven's Gate: The **Porta Coeli Church** is San Germán's – and arguably Puerto Rico's – greatest architectural inheritance. Founded in 1606, it is the oldest church under the United States flag (not that one flies too conspicuously over its facade). It is also one of only a handful of Gothic churches in the western world. The others are in San Juan, Colombia and Mexico – it is one of the great glories of Spanish colonization that the conquest came about early enough to assure that this neo-medieval style, which peppered all the countries of Europe with some of the greatest monuments to man's artistry, could also flourish in the New World.

Porta Coeli means "heaven's gate" and, indeed, its portals are of great importance in its artistry. It's a squat little whitewashed building standing at the top of a broad, spreading stairway of scrabbly brick and mortar. Its doors are of beautiful *ausubo*, a once-common Puerto Rican hardwood, and are larger than the walls of many New York City apartments. These are framed by an austere pediment, above which is a battened skylight of the same wood.

Inside, the pews and altar are all original, with embellishment. The altar piece was painted by the first great Puerto

Rican artist, José Campeche, in the late 18th century, a fact that would indicate the church was fairly well-established as an historical landmark even by then. Porta Coeli overlooks one of the most beautifully landscaped plazas in Puerto Rico, with its terraced benches and beautifully groomed trees.

Name that church: San Germán, like Ponce, is a two-plaza town, and its second, the **Plaza Mario Quiñones**, is no less impressive than that overlooked by Porta Coeli, with the same lovely walks, period lamplights and marvelous topiary. But it also has a church to rival Porta Coeli in appeal, if not in age. The **Church of San Germán de Auxerre** commemorates the French saint who is the town's patron. Its steeple does not face the plaza directly, but has its facade on a nearby side street. While less important than much of San Germán in historical terms, it dominates the town, and is particularly impressive when viewed from the surrounding hills on a sunny day.

Ancient homes: San Germán's oldest

attractions – the two churches, in particular – have always captured the attention of visitors, but few have stopped to examine the general layout and ambience of this ancient town with the rigor and delight that tourists have always brought to San Juan and Ponce. This of course is due in some degree to the fact that San Germán remained so small until very recently that it cannot boast a great number of typically Puerto Rican wrought–iron and stone residences, which tend to be most attractive in long rows in large neighborhoods.

But San Germán has a treasure trove of more recent architectural masterpieces, as Jorge Rigau and others at San Juan's Colegio de Arquitectos have recently brought to public attention. Marvelous haciendas of the late 19th-century coffee barons are abundant, and demonstrate a style which, while it can be seen throughout the southwest – in Yauco, for example, is as much San Germán's own as Porta Coeli.

These houses must be entered to be appreciated, as much of their charm lies in the way the interior spaces are divided. Beautiful *mediopunto* carvings – delicate lacy half-screens of snaking wood – create conceptual divisions between rooms without actually putting up a substantial physical barrier. Some of these are astounding harbingers of art nouveau, as are the simple and sinuous stencilings which grace the walls of many houses.

Multinational students: San Germán's **Inter-American University** is a hive of 8,000 students tucked into one of the oldest cities in the Americas. The university infuses the place with a cultural spirit that saves San Germán from being one of those cities which is cultured only so long as the tourists stay around. Its multinational student body and faculty is one of the most important sources of scholarly information in this fascinating town. Those interested in understanding more deeply the past and present of the place should take advantage of its many cultural offerings. In a town the size of San Germán, the university and its students have considerable impact.

Left, Plaza Mario Quiñones. Right, Porta Coeli church.

SOUTHWEST TIP

Puerto Rico is blessed with several phosphorescent bays, but none as renowned as **Parguera**. Around this southwestern curiosity has developed a town just as curious, and a farrago of fascinating things to do.

Those who arrive in Parguera town without realizing that the famous bay is somewhat east will be surprised by the hubbub and urbanity of the place. Parguera is not a quiet little nature-seekers' haven by any means; it's a jampacked, neon-lit beehive of hucksters and fastfood joints, which on summer nights is alive with partying youngsters and thrill-seeking tourists. This is not to say the place is spoiled; it serves the very useful function of diverting the inevitable crowds from the area's more delicate attractions.

Boats ply the waters between the village and the bay itself with reassuring frequency. For a few dollars, you'll most likely get an hour in the flying Caribbean spindrift and one of the rare opportunities Puerto Rico affords to make use of a warm sweater. Leaving the docks, cruises run through the yachts and fishing boats of Parguera's poorly sheltered harbor and past a tiny chain of islets whose focus is **Isla Magueyes**, home to a large colony of lizards.

As cruise boats enter the bay itself, their wakes turn an eerie pale-green. Captains invite the passengers to scoop their hands over the gunwales and into the water to produce odd, remarkable patterns. A bucket is generally brought on board for the curious to play with, and in cupped palms water breaks into shapes resembling splattering mercury.

The phosphorescence is produced by billions of micro-organisms which belong to the family of dinoflagellates known as *pyrodinium bahamense*. Try to see this unique phenomenon on a cloudy night with a light breeze, when no other light sources muddle the brilliance of the waters, and wavelets make ever-changing patterns on the surface.

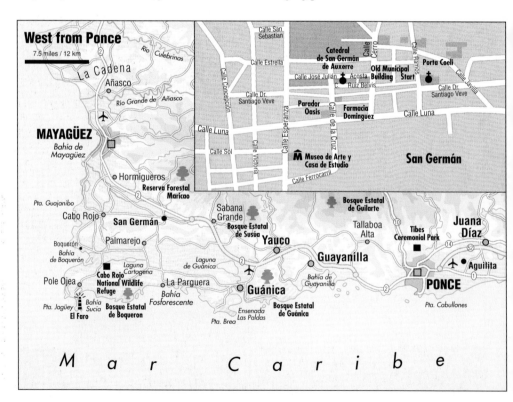

To the point: Surrounded by coral-studded Caribbean waters, bathed in dry tropical heat year-round and sculpted into an odd network of cliffs, lagoons, promontories and swamps by fickle surfs and tides, the *municipio* of **Cabo Rojo** shows Puerto Rico's seaside landscape at its eeriest and most alluring.

Stretching south along 18 miles of coast from Mayagüez, this area is among the remotest on the island; whether approaching from Ponce or from Mayagüez, one notices the landscape growing drier and more hummocky, the population more sparse and the scenery more beautiful.

For those to whom the name "Cabo Rojo" has been made synonymous with isolated retreats and breathtaking vistas, **Cabo Rojo Town** can come as something of a disappointment. It is unquestionably a quaint and pretty town, however, and full of history. Its 10,000 residents are well up on local lore, including tales of the infamous Spanish buccaneer Roberto Confresí, who made this part of the island his home during 17th-century raids on European merchant ships.

Four and a half miles (7½ km) northwest of the town lies **Laguna Joyuda,** a mangrove swamp which is a sanctuary for birds native to the region. Mangroves are among the most hospitable of environments for semi-tropical bird life, and Cabo Rojo boasts them in higher concentration than any other area in the western half of Puerto Rico. This 300-acre expanse is home to herons, martins and pelicans, including the lovely maroon pelican. The lagoon itself is full of fish, and is phosphorescent on moonless nights, due to a preponderance of the dinoflagellate *pyrodinium bahamense* here as in Parguera

A battery of beaches: Everyone in Puerto Rico has his favorite beach, but **Playa Buye**, just southwest of Cabo Rojo on Route 307, gets more votes than many. With its wispy rows of pine hooking around a promontory to the bay known as **Puerto Real**, and with pleasant views of the tiny village of Elizabeth across the water, Buye makes up in charm what

El Combate, Cabo Rojo.

it lacks in size. The landscape changes with shocking suddenness just south of Buye, as the cliffs of **Punta Guanaquilla** give way to the swamps and mangroves of the tiny **Laguna Guanaquilla**. The cliffs and lagoon are best reached either by making the ¾-mile (1-km) walk south or by taking the dirt road that leads out of the tiny settlement of **Boca Prieta** at the southern end of Buye.

Competing beaches: Seven miles south of Cabo Rojo on Route 4 and 101, **Boquerón** is a fishing port of staggering beauty. Like Laguna Joyuda, it is blessed with a mangrove forest which shelters some of Puerto Rico's loveliest birds – the Laguna Rincón and surrounding forests have been designated a bird sanctuary as one of the three parts of the **Boquerón Nature Reserve**.

But it is hardly bird-watching that brings most visitors to the town. For Boquerón sits at the mouth of a 3-mile-long bay whose placid, coral-flecked waters and broad sands backed by palm groves make **Playa Boquerón** almost without question the finest beach on the island. In a place where regional rivalries are as intense as in Puerto Rico, the fact that even some Luquillo residents will admit as much is significant.

Every weekend, fishermen bring their fresh catches to Boquerón to sell to the bathers. The cabins around Boquerón's beach are popular among weekenders; to rent one, contact the Department of Recreation and Sports in San Juan at least four months in advance.

Tucked in Puerto Rico's southwestern corner at the end of Route 301, a circuitous 6 miles south of Boquerón, **El Combate** is yet another beach of renown, with a charming row of fishing shacks and a crowded jetty.

But, to the point: Route 301 travels even farther south past **Pole Oleja**, a not-terribly inspiring salt settlement which is worth only a short look. Two miles south, however, at the southwest-ernmost extremity of Puerto Rico, is the crowning glory of Cabo Rojo and one of the most scenic spots in the entire Caribbean. This is **Punta Jagüey**, a kidney-shaped rock outcrop connected to land by a narrow isthmus and straddling two lovely bays, the **Bahia Salinas** and the **Bahia Succia**.

Herons and eelgrass: Here too is a nature reserve of grand proportions; both the peninsula and the surrounding waters are protected as part of the same Boquerón system that embraces Laguna Rincón. But there is more to Punta Jagüey than herons and eelgrass. **Cabo Rojo Lighthouse** – if you can look past the graffiti that has unfortunately obscured its sides – is a breathtaking specimen of Spanish colonial architecture, with its low-lying, pale-sided main building and squat, hexagonal light tower. It perches atop dun-colored cliffs at the very extremity of the peninsula and commands views of almost 300 degrees of Caribbean.

With wide-open prospects to both east and west, the lighthouse is at its most awe-inspiring when its walls are given a faint blush by either sunrise or sunset. It's more likely you'll see the latter; many trips to Cabo Rojo are conceived as daytrips and somehow carry on into the evening.

Below, Boquerón Beach. Right, selling oysters.

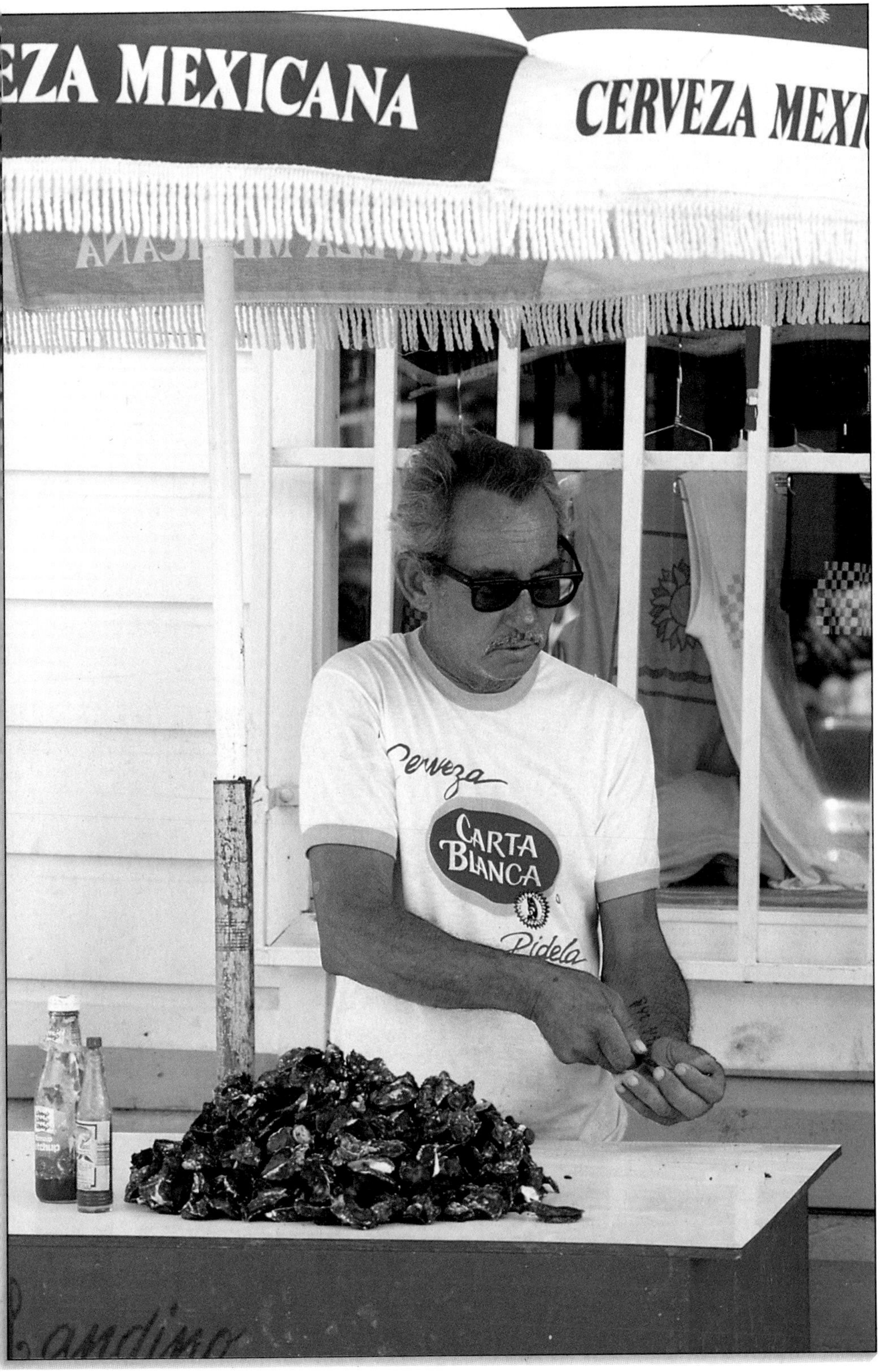
EZA MEXICANA
CERVEZA MEXI
Cerveza
CARTA BLANCA
Pidela

MAYAGÜEZ

The third largest of Puerto Rico's three major cities is the only one which can claim the sort of cosmopolitan-cum-hedonistic lifestyle that makes a certain type of traveler fall in love with a city. San Juan and Ponce have other, perhaps deeper, charms, but both are a bit too hardworking and serious to compete with the relaxing atmosphere of their little sister out west. There's something about **Mayagüez's** modernism – this is not to say lack of history – which lends an irresponsible, vaguely Californian ethos to life there. Add to this beautiful ocean breezes and the best swimming and surfing on the island, and one is left with a holiday spot for those who wish to relax and be self-indulgent, rather than those who want to do a great deal of sightseeing or culture seeking.

This would tend to draw droves of adipose *norteamericanos* and, to be fair, Mayagüez does share with Vieques the distinction of being the greatest hangout for professional expatriates in Puerto Rico. But the beach-bums here tend to be of a more contemplative bent. For all its charms, Mayagüez remains difficult to get to. Those who reach it tend to be of superior mettle, and guzzle the local India beer with the vengeance only those who have worked hard for their holidays can understand.

Fishy business: Not all is beer and skittles in this western metropolis; in fact, the isolation of those who engage in high living from those who are stuck making a living is in large degree responsible for the particular pace of life in Mayagüez. Pared down to its most basic, Mayagüez is a fish-packing town with a university. The town lives on tuna, at least indirectly; over 60 percent of the tuna eaten in the United States is tinned at Mayagüez, and a substantial number of residents make their living off the stuff.

Since Section 936 funding has lured so many foreign (primarily US) businesses to Puerto Rico, the city has also taken a larger share of Puerto Rico's monolithic pharmaceutical industry from Arecibo.

Mayagüez's College, located on Route 108, is an outpost of the **University of Puerto Rico**. It's primarily an engineering and agricultural college, so the ferment over issues political and literary which is so much a part of the University of Puerto Rico in Río Piedras doesn't really penetrate much here. But the college is right next to one of the finest places for learning that Puerto Rico has to offer, the **Tropical Agricultural Research Station**. Run by the US Department of Agriculture, these gardens, built on the site of a former plantation, boast one of the largest collections of tropical and semi-tropical plants in the world. Nearby is the new and somewhat hyper-modern **Mayagüez Mall**, a scaled-down version of San Juan's Plaza Las Américas.

Ladies of Barcelona: All this is only about a half-mile north of Mayagüez's main plaza, the **Plaza Colón**. A statue dead-center commemorates Christopher Columbus. Round about are 16 differ-

Left, tuna plant, Mayagüez. **Right**, cleaning the fish.

TUNA TERRITORY

Driving along Mayagüez Bay, you can literally smell Puerto Rico's tuna industry a mile away. The stench is an unpleasant but necessary part of life in this small metropolis, where, despite the industry's gradual decline in recent years, thousands of jobs still depend on the export of canned tuna-fish to the United States.

From the road, you can make out a rusty chain-link fence separating the sprawling operations of rivals Bumble Bee International and StarKist Caribe, two of the world's largest tuna processors who between them supply about half the canned tuna in the United States.

The fence ends at the water's edge, where both companies, in identical but separate operations, unload frozen tuna from different holds of the same vessel. The companies are here mainly because of Section 936 of the United States Internal Revenue Code. This is a tax holiday that exempts them from federal income tax on local profits.

The canneries aren't open to the public;

even local journalists have a hard time getting in, so secret and competitive is the business. Traditionally, Bumble Bee controls the market in albacore tuna, while StarKist's strength lies in yellowfin and skipjack. In the early 1990s, the industry suffered a major setback when controversy erupted over the strangulation of thousands of dolphins in tuna nets. Since the mammals swim mainly with yellowfin, adopting so-called "dolphin-safe" policies meant giving up nearly 300,000 tons of yellowfin tuna annually. While pleasing environmentalists, this policy has led to higher costs and smaller profit margins.

Even before the dolphin-safe issue arose, Puerto's tuna industry was being decimated by low-wage Far East competition. In 1986, the island had five canneries employing close to 8,000 people. Today, there are only three, with a combined workforce of 5,080.

StarKist's 600,000-sq. ft Mayagüez facility remains the world's largest tuna cannery, though employment there has dropped from 4,300 to 3,500. Employment at its next-door neighbor, Bumble Bee, was slashed from 2,000 to 1,200 shortly after the company became a subsidiary of Thailand's Unicorp in 1991. And in Ponce, Caribe Tuna – owned by Mitsubishi Foods of Japan – has reduced its workers from 800 to 380.

The Van Camp packing-plant in Ponce closed in 1991 after an Indonesian firm, P.T. Mantrust, bought the company and transferred its facilities to American Samoa. Another cannery, Neptune Packing, was closed the same year by its Japanese owners, Mitsui & Co. Inc.

In 1993, StarKist, Bumble Bee and Caribe Tuna exported a combined 181,000 tons of processed tuna to the United States east coast, where it sold for around $475 million. Tuna workers earn about $5.30 an hour plus fringe benefits, about 12 times the average hourly wage of their rivals in the Far East.

In addition to much higher labor costs, canneries here must contend with stricter environmental regulations, high transportation costs and greater distance from the world's leading fisheries. For this reason, industry experts say that if the United States Congress ever abolished Section 936 tax incentives – as it has often proposed doing – the three remaining canneries would simply pack up and leave Puerto Rico. ■ **Unloading frozen tuna.**

ent bronze statues of courtly ladies brought from Barcelona. The ground in the plaza is as smooth and shiny as an ice-skating rink, and the buildings around it are dignified and imposing, particularly the neo-Corinthian **Alcaldía**, with its lovely crimson and white facade.

There is plenty more happening around Mayagüez. The **Mayagüez Zoo**, about 15 miles outside of town, is one of those zoos that is something like a nature park, as animals roam about not in cages but in an environment as close to their native habitats as is possible in a climate where it almost never drops below 70°F (21°C) or rises above 80°F (27°C). It's an enjoyable family place, as small town zoos always are, with such wild animals as ringtailed lemurs and Bengal tigers.

As it was: Mayagüez is not without history. The native Taíno Indians found the place every bit as alluring as today's beach-bums and pharmaceutical companies, and when Columbus landed here on his second voyage to the Caribbean,

he found a great number of welcoming natives. The name Mayagüez means "place of many streams" and the confluence of so many tributaries gives an open-to-the-sea feeling to the city. One of these, the Río Yagüez, gives the city its name. Should the Spanish and Taíno constituents of this odd body of water be translated into similar English, we'd be left with the infinitely descriptive moniker of the "Water River."

Devastation: As a Spanish settlement, however, the city dates only from the end of the 18th century, when fishermen found the riches of the Mona Passage too alluring to pass up. Tragically, Mayagüez's history under Spanish dominion has been all but lost to us. The earthquake which rocked the entire western part of the island in 1918 fairly devastated Mayagüez, with the result that the town was almost depopulated.

Just 5 miles south of Mayagüez is the tiny *municipio* of **Hormigueros**, which is a suburb only in the sense that it is below its parent city on the map. This is a city with the pace of the Northwest and

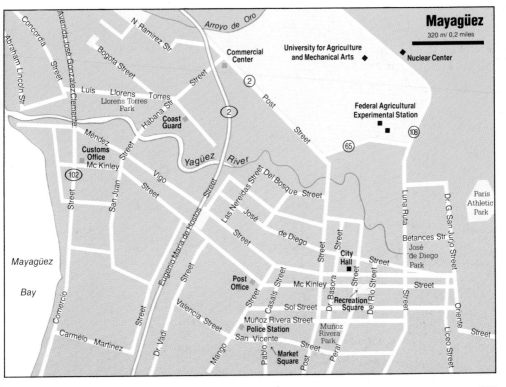

the layout of a Cordillera town, with narrow, winding streets and one of the finest cathedrals on the island.

The **Cathedral of Our Lady of Montserrat** is at once awesome and unassuming. Bone-white towers of varying dimensions arise to domes of crimson topped with austere white crucifixes of wood. Elevated slightly above the town, it appears to soar into the sky with an effect that is, oddly enough, best appreciated on a cloudy day. Yet its proximity to the streets which surround it, its everyday color scheme and something in the ordinary way with which Hormiguerans go about life with such a treasure in their midst keeps the cathedral a friendly looking place with no pretensions.

Hormigueros itself is worth a day-excursion from Mayagüez, if only to catch a glimpse of the cathedral, have a cool can of India in a side street bar and do a bit of shopping on the city's main avenues.

Untouched island: Throughout the Caribbean, it's hard not to feel that, however beautiful the landscape may be, it must *really* have been heart-stopping before the European settlers arrived. There are still a few places that the hand of civilization has not reached, though, and one of them, the tiny **Isle of Mona**, belongs to Puerto Rico. Stuck 45 miles out to sea, halfway to the Dominican Republic in the Mona Passage, this rugged island of 25 sq. miles is a haven for some of the oddest and most interesting wildlife in the Antilles, and remains as bizarre and uninhabited as it is difficult to reach.

Protected beauty: Mona is now protected by the Department of Natural Resources, which supervises the use of Cabo Rojo and other spots of great scenic beauty on the west coast. Nobody lives there now, but Mona has actually had a long history of inhabitation. Christopher Columbus found Taíno Indians there when he landed on the island, and Spanish settlers visited for many years in hopes of finding livable and pleasant spots to settle. For centuries it was the stronghold for some of the **Mayagüez.**

most notorious of European and Puerto Rican pirates.

It is rumored that treasure lies buried on the island to this day, and perhaps it does. For a brief period a century ago, certain prospectors carried out a brilliant scheme to mine not gold, not silver, not copper from the caves of this remote island, but... well, bat-droppings. For fertilizer. The scheme never got off the ground. Nor did an ambitious 1973 plan by Fomento, Puerto Rico's economic development agency, to turn Mona into a major petrochemicals and refining center. Outraged environmentalists stopped the proposal in its tracks. Since then, only a few naturalists and hermits have visited, as the scheme never flourished.

As they left it: The landscape these solitary types have found is reported to be astounding. Except for a solitary lighthouse on a remote promontory, Mona is much as the Taínos left it. Cliffs 200 feet high ring the tiny island. The cliffs are laced with a cave network which some say rivals that of the Camuy.

Much of the island's ground is covered by small cacti which resemble a miniature version of Arizona's organ pipe cactus, and tiny barrel cacti are common as well.

Some of the vegetation on the island is known nowhere else in the world. The fauna is even more astounding. Here are found the biggest lizards in Puerto Rico, ugly iguanas growing to 3 feet long. Besides an extensive variety of gulls, there lives on Mona a red-footed bird beloved by visitors and known disrespectfully as the "booby."

The perils of travel: There are those who would claim that anyone who wished to visit Mona could be called a booby as well. Those hardy souls who are not dissuaded would be best advised to charter a boat or private plane in Mayagüez. Apparently, planes can be chartered from San Juan's Isla Grande Airport as well. Official information on hiking trails and on the island's topography is hard to come by, but try writing to the **Departmento de Recursos Naturales** in San Juan.

INSIGHT GUIDES
Travel Tips

So, you're getting away from it all.

Just make sure you can get back.

AT&T Access Numbers
Dial the number of the country you're in to reach AT&T.

ANGUILLA	1-800-872-2881	**CHILE**	**00◇-0312**	HONDURAS†	123
ANTIGUA (Public Card Phones)	#1	**COLOMBIA**	**980-11-0010**	JAMAICA††	0-800-872-2881
ARGENTINA◆	001-800-200-1111	*COSTA RICA	114	MEXICO◇◇◇	95-800-462-4240
BAHAMAS	**1-800-872-2881**	**CURACAO**	**001-800-872-2881**	MONTSERRAT†	1-800-872-2881
BARBADOS†	1-800-872-2881	DOMINICA	1-800-872-2881	**NICARAGUA**	**174**
BELIZE◆	555	DOMINICAN REP.††	11-22	PANAMA	109
BERMUDA†	1-800-872-2881	ECUADOR†	119	PARAGUAY†	0081-800
*BOLIVIA	0-800-1112	*EL SALVADOR	190	ST. KITTS/NEVIS	1-800-872-2881
BONAIRE	**001-800-872-2881**	GRENADA†	1-800-872-2881	**ST. MAARTEN**	**001-800-872-2881**
BRAZIL	**000-8010**	*GUATEMALA	190	**SURINAME**	**156**
BRITISH V. I.	1-800-872-2881	***GUYANA††**	**165**	URUGUAY	00-0410
CAYMAN ISLANDS	1-800-872-2881	HAITI†	001-800-972-2883	*VENEZUELA	80-011-120

Countries in bold face permit country-to-country calling in addition to calls to the U.S. **World Connect**℠ prices consist of **USADirect**® rates plus an additional charge based on the country you are calling. Collect calling available to the U.S. only. *Public phones require deposit of coin or phone card. ◇ Await second dial tone. †May not be available from every phone. ††Collect calling only. ◆ Not available from public phones. ◇◇◇ When calling from public phones, use phones marked "Ladatel". ©1994 AT&T.

Here's a travel tip that will make it easy to call back to the States. Dial the access number for the country you're in to get English-speaking AT&T operators or voice prompts. Minimize hotel telephone surcharges too.

If all the countries you're visiting aren't listed above, call **1 800 241-5555** for a free wallet card with all AT&T access numbers. Easy international calling from AT&T. **TrueWorld Connections.**

AT&T

TRAVEL TIPS

GETTING THERE

BY AIR

San Juan's **Luís Muñoz Marín International Airport**, just west of the city center in Isla Verde, is one of the largest airports in the Caribbean, serving not only as Puerto Rico's main port of tourist entry but also as a stopping point for most US and European flights to the Virgin Islands and other Caribbean islands. The most important international carriers serving San Juan include American Airlines, Avianca, Copa, Delta Airlines, Dominicana de Aviacíon, Iberia, LIAT, Lufthansa, TWA, United and Viasa. Sometimes known as Isla Verde, the airport terminal is a sunny and florid two-level structure.

Free buses run to most car rental agencies not in the airport, and those operated by the Metropolitan Bus Authority run to various parts of the city for only a small charge. Taxi fares are determined on a per-mile basis, with an initial charge and an additional charge for luggage.

AIRLINES

The following airline offices are in Puerto Rico. The area code is (0101) 809. Numbers preceded by 800 are available on the island and in the US only and are toll-free.

Aeropostal, tel: 721-2166
American, tel: 749-1747
British Airways, tel: 725-1575
Canadian Int'l, tel: 791-4730
Carnival, tel: 259-1010
Copa, tel: 722-6969
Delta, tel: 721-1011
Dominicana, tel: 724-7100
Flamenco, tel: 723-8100
Iberia, tel: 721-5630
Kiwi, tel: 724-7570
LACSA, tel: 724-3330
LIAT, tel: 791-3838
Lufthansa, tel: 723-9553
Mexicana, tel: 722-8212
Northwest, tel: (800) 225-2525
Sunaire Express, tel: 791-4744
TWA, tel: (800) 221-2000
United, tel: (800) 538-2929
US Air, tel: (800) 842-5374
Vieques Air Link, tel: 722-3736

BY SEA

While regular passenger service to Puerto Rico is rare, cruise ships are commonplace. San Juan is the most popular cruise port in the Caribbean, receiving over 1 million visitors annually. Several modern "tourism piers" have been constructed at the harborside in Old San Juan, with the result that most cruise companies plying the South Atlantic make at least an afternoon stop in San Juan.

TRAVEL ESSENTIALS

VISAS & PASSPORTS

No visa or passport is required for US citizens entering Puerto Rico from the United States. Those with permanent residence, however, are advised to bring their green cards in order to avoid occasional hassles by US immigration authorities upon leaving for mainland flights. Foreign nationals are required to present the same documentation required for entry into the continental US.

MONEY MATTERS

All business in Puerto Rico is transacted in US dollars. Owing to its isolation from main supply lines, Puerto Rico is slightly more expensive than the mainland. Inflation is not presently a problem, and hovers under 5 percent.

Puerto Rico has no sales tax. There are taxes on alcohol and cigarettes, though these are included in marked prices and do not appear as surcharges.

CREDIT CARDS

Most restaurants and hotels in well-traveled areas honor American Express, MasterCard and Visa, Carte Blanche, Diner's Club. Ideal and Discover cards are accepted at a smaller number of establishments. The Lufthansa card and the Hilton International card pass muster at a handful of the larger resorts.

There are two American Express Travel Services on the island:

Agencias Soler, 1035 Ashford Ave, Condado, tel: 725-0960.
Agencias Soler, 8 W. Méndez Vigo St, Mayagüez, tel: 834-3300.

A Wise Man Never Thinks How Far He's Come. He Thinks How Far He Can Still Travel.

REMY XO BECAUSE LIFE IS WHAT YOU MAKE IT

Swatch. The others just watch.

seahorse/fall winter 94-95

shockproof
splashproof
priceproof
boreproof
swiss made

swatch
SCUBA 200

WHAT TO WEAR

Puerto Rican dressing is extremely casual. Jeans and knit trousers are common legwear. So are shorts, though primarily only among tourists, as locals tend to shun them. Only in a very small number of clubs are jackets and ties required, and businessmen often remove their jackets in the course of the workday. Men frequently wear *guayaberas* – long-sleeve shirts, often cotton, with intricate lace work on the front – as formal wear. Colorful, medium-length dresses are versatile evening wear for women.

Anything more than a light sweater is seldom necessary, even on winter nights in the Cordillera. However, some kind of sunscreen will be necessary for those who plan to spend even a minimal amount of time outdoors. An umbrella will come in useful, especially in late summer on the island's northern coast.

CUSTOMS

Customs regulations resemble those of the United States, and are carried out with similar thoroughness. It is illegal to transport perishable foods, plants or animals into or out of Puerto Rico except with prior permission. This stipulation applies to those traveling to and from the United States as well. Duty-free shops are open for all international flights, and for flights to the United States and US possessions in the Caribbean.

GETTING ACQUAINTED

Puerto Rican motto: *Joannes est nomen ejus* (John is his Name)
Puerto Rican song: *La Borinqueña*
Puerto Rican flower: *Amatola*

GOVERNMENT & ECONOMY

Puerto Rico's official status is *Estado Libre Asociado,* or "Free Associated State." It is most commonly referred to as the "Commonwealth of Puerto Rico." Under an agreement which dates from 1950, Puerto Ricans are American citizens, with almost all the economic and personal rights and responsibilities pertaining thereto. At the head of the island's government is an elected governor; Puerto Rico has an elected Senate and House of Representatives, which work very much like the American system.

While Puerto Rico has presidential primaries, Puerto Ricans are not permitted to vote in national elections. However, they are represented in the US Congress by a resident commissioner who can sit on committes but cannot vote. Puerto Rican residents pay no federal income tax, while Section 936 of the US Internal Revenue Code provides economic incentives for US businesses that invest in Puerto Rico.

Manufacturing is still considered the largest sector of the local economy. Puerto Rico is the world's largest producer of pharmaceuticals. Petrochemicals are another strong industry, as is tourism. Puerto Rico remains the banking center for most of the Caribbean.

The island's per capita income is $6,300 lower than that of any of the United States. Twenty-three percent of the work force is employed by the government. The island's gross domestic product amounts to nearly $24 billion, by far the largest in the Caribbean and one of the largest in Latin America.

GEOGRAPHY

Puerto Rico is an island of 3,421 sq. miles (8,895 sq. km) facing the Atlantic on the north and the Caribbean on the south. It is the smallest of the Greater Antilles, running 100 miles (165 km) east-to-west and 35 miles (58 km) north-to-south. Three offshore islands of significant size complete its territory: Vieques and Culebra, geologically and geographically part of the Virgin Islands; and Mona, an uninhabited islet halfway between Puerto Rico and the Dominican Republic in the Mona Passage. The Puerto Rico trench, which runs 30,000 feet (10,000 meters) deep just north of the island, is the deepest part of the Atlantic.

The island itself has been described as "a mountain range surrounded by sugar cane." While this is not exactly fair, it is true that very little of the island is flat. The Cordillera Central ("central spine"), a mountain range whose peaks reach well over 3,000 feet (1,000 meters), takes up most of the island's area and is surrounded on all sides by foothills. To the northeast, odd haystack-shaped limestone formations make up the karst country, a unique and fascinating landscape of rock cones and caves.

Puerto Rico is ringed by palm-lined, white-sand beaches and by coral reefs, and is veined with rivers and streams of all sizes. The island has no natural lakes. San Juan is one of the finest natural harbors in the Caribbean.

TIME ZONES

Puerto Rico is located in the Atlantic Time Zone, four hours behind GMT and one hour ahead of Eastern Standard Time. In summer, there is no time difference between Puerto Rico and the US East Coast, since Puerto Rico does not observe Daylight Savings Time.

Thus, barring time adjustments in other countries, when it is 12 noon in Puerto Rico it is:

6am in Hawaii
8am in California
10am in Chicago
11am in New York, Boston and Miami
4pm in London
5pm in Bonn, Madrid, Paris and Rome
7pm in Athens and Cairo
8pm in Moscow
9.30pm in Bombay
11pm in Bangkok
midnight in Singapore, Taiwan and Hong Kong
1am (the next day) in Tokyo
2am (the next day) in Sydney

CLIMATE

Puerto Rico has one of the most pleasant and unvarying climates in the world, with daily highs almost invariably at 70–85°F (21–29°C). The island is at its wettest and hottest in August, with 7 inches (18 cm) the average monthly rainfall and 81°F (27°C) the average daily high. Especially during the rainy season, sudden late-afternoon squalls are not infrequent. Regional variations are noticeable: Ponce and the southern coast are generally warmer and drier than San Juan and the north. Weather is coldest in the higher altitudes of the Cordillera, where the lowest temperature in the history of the island was recorded near Barranquitas: 39°F (4°C). Average daily high temperatures for San Juan are:

January	(75°F/24°C)
February	(75°F/24°C)
March	(76°F/24°C)
April	(78°F/26°C)
May	(79°F/26°C)
June	(81°F/27°C)
July	(81°F/27°C)
August	(81°F/27°C)
September	(81°F/27°C)
October	(81°F/27°C)
November	(79°F/26°C)
December	(77°F/25°C)

TIPPING

Puerto Rico has a service economy resembling that of the United States, and this means tipping for most services received. Follow the American rules of thumb: 15 percent in restaurants, including *fondas* and *colmados* but not including fast-food joints; 10 percent in bars; 10–15 percent for cab-drivers, hairdressers and other services. Fifty cents per bag is a good rule for hotel porters, and a few bucks should keep the person who cleans your room happy.

WEIGHTS & MEASURES

While Puerto Rico is nominally in accord with the United States' use of English measures, most weights and measures tend to be metric. Most conspicuously, road distances are in kilometers, gasoline is sold by the liter and meats sold in kilograms. Yet speed limits are still in miles per hour.

BUSINESS HOURS

BANKING

Puerto Rico is the banking center of the Caribbean Basin and as such has almost all of the leading North American banks, as well as many European and native Puerto Rican ones. It is harder than one might expect in this much-touristed island to change money, especially outside of the major cities; it is probably best for foreigners to buy their traveler's checks in US dollars.

Most banks are open Monday through Friday from 9am to 2.30pm, with some remaining open on Saturday mornings.

FESTIVALS

Almost every holiday is the occasion for a festival in Puerto Rico, many of them legislated, others informal. Every town has its patron saint, and every saint his or her festival. These, known as *patronales*, are the biggest events of the year in their respective towns. A complete list of these would be impossible to compile, but the most famous is probably Loíza's **Fiesta de Santiago Apostól** in July. The largest is certainly San Juan's wild festival in late June.

A not-very-authentic, but somewhat interesting, year-long festival has been established by the Puerto Rican Tourism Company. The **"Le Lo Lai Festival"** is for those who happen to arrive in a bad season for real festivals, and happen to stay in hotels which participate in the Le Lo Lai program. Le Lo Lai generally involves nightly shows of Puerto Rican music and dance programs staged in hotels. Consult the Tourism Company for details.

The annual public holidays are:

1 January	New Year's Day
6 January	Three Kings' Day
10 January	Birth of Eugenio Maria de Hostos
17 January	Martin Luther King Day
21 February	George Washington's Birthday
22 March	Abolition of Slavery
1 April	Good Friday
18 April	Birth of José de Diego
30 May	Memorial Day
4 July	US Independence Day
18 July	Birth of Luís Muñoz Rivera
25 July	Constitution Day
5 September	Labor Day
12 October	Columbus Day

11 November	Veterans' Day
19 November	Discovery of Puerto Rico
3rd Thursday	
in November	Thanksgiving Day
25 December	Christmas

COMMUNICATIONS

MEDIA

Puerto Ricans are avid readers of periodical literature, and the national dailies, published in San Juan, cover the entire spectrum of political opinion. Of the Spanish papers, *El Nuevo Día* is probably the most popular, a meaty tabloid with special features and book excerpts well worth the quarter.

El Vocero is a slim paper with more local, sensational news. *Claridad*, the pro-independence newspaper, is provocative reading and popular among the youth of the left. *The San Juan Star*, in English, concentrates heavily on North American news and serves as a sort of Caribbean *International Herald Tribune*.

A host of local papers rounds off the island's periodicals. Puerto Rico produces few good magazines, but gets most of the weeklies from the United States and Spain. American newspapers are available here on the day of publication: in Spanish, *Diario de las Americas*, published in Miami; in English, *The New York Times*, *The New York Post*, *The Miami Herald* and *The Wall Street Journal*.

Puerto Rico has more than 100 radio stations, including the English-language WOSO (1030 on the AM dial) which provides hourly news, weather and sports "throughout the San Juan metroplex."

In eastern Puerto Rico, English-language radio stations can be received from the US Virgin Islands. The island also has half a dozen TV stations of its own.

POSTAL SERVICES

Puerto Rican postal services are administered by the US Postal Service. Regulations and tariffs are the same as those on the mainland. Stamps may be purchased at any post office; most are open from 8am to 5pm, Monday through Friday and from 8am to noon on Saturdays. Stamps may also be purchased from vending machines located in hotels, stores and airports.

The USPS-Authorized Abbreviation for Puerto Rico is PR.

TELEPHONE & TELEX

Coin-operated telephones are common and cost a dime for local calls. Deposit the coin first. When you hear the dial tone, you may dial the seven-digit number. If the call is long-distance within Puerto Rico, extra charges will apply. For calls to the US Virgin Islands, Dominican Republic or anywhere in the English-speaking Caribbean, dial "1-809" and the number. For other long-distance calls to the US and Canada, you must dial "1," then the area code, then the number. An operator will tell you how much to deposit. If you wish to place a call through an operator, simply dial "0." Directions are usually printed on the phone, and are always printed in the first pages of the phone directory.

The phone directories in Puerto Rico are in Spanish, with a special section of blue pages in English providing commercial and government telephone numbers and giving translations of the Spanish headings under which information can be found.

Telegraph facilities are available through Western Union or telex. Western Union telegraphs and cash transfers arrive at food stores of the Pueblo chain.

EMERGENCIES

SECURITY & CRIME

In recent years, the crime rate in Puerto Rico has skyrocketed and the annual murder rate is approaching 900. It is a place with high unemployment and a tourist population which is often gullible and vulnerable. Travelers would be wise to take certain precautions.

Nevertheless, petty theft and confidence scams are more prevalent in Puerto Rico than violent crimes. Always lock your rooms, especially in smaller lodgings. Never leave luggage unattended or out of sight. Most hotels will store bags at the front desk, as will many restaurants and shops. Never leave valuables in your room. If possible, leave your room key at the front desk when you leave your hotel or guest house for any length of time.

Always lock automobiles, regardless of whether you have left any valuables inside, as the car radios which come with most rentals are extremely valuable, easily saleable and much coveted by thieves.

As traveler's checks are accepted all over Puerto Rico, there is no reason to carry more than the cash you need. For emergencies in the San Juan metro area, call 911. The police can also be reached at 343-2020.

MEDICAL SERVICES

Puerto Rico's health care resembles that of the United States in that it has no *de jure* national health service, and in that the sick are cared for on a pay-as-you-go basis.

In practice, however, Puerto Rico's health care is administered on a far more lenient basis than in the United States. Fees are in general much cheaper, and the fact that many Puerto Ricans receive treatment under insurance policies means that being hospitalized for injury is far less of a financial nightmare than it is in the continental United States. Most hospitals have 24-hour emergency rooms but, if possible, check the yellow pages of the telephone book under *Servicio Emergencia de Hospitales.*

Puerto Rico is full of competent medical professionals. If you could choose where to fall ill, you'd doubtless choose San Juan, as the number of universities and clinics there make it full of doctors and medical personnel. Still, facilities in other areas, though often old and disheartening at a first visit, are generally run by physicians and nurses as capable and concerned as any in the Caribbean.

Below are listed some of the larger hospitals with emergency rooms and some of the more popular (not necessarily 24-hour) drugstores in San Juan. For listings in provincial cities, check the yellow pages in the telephone book.

HOSPITALS

Ashford Presbyterian Community Hospital, tel: 721-2160.
De Diego Hospital, 310 De Diego Ave, Stop 22, Santurce, tel: 721-8181.
Hospital Nuestra Señora de Guadelupe, 435 Ponce de León, Hato Rey, tel: 754-0909.
Metropolitan Hospital, 1785 Carr. 21, Las Lomas, P.V., Río Piedras, tel: 783-6200.
Hospital Auxilio Mutuo, Hato Rey, tel: 758-2000.
Hospital San Pablo, Bayamón, tel: 747-4747.
Hospital Pavia, Santurce, tel: 727-6060.

PHARMACIES

OLD SAN JUAN: Puerto Rico Drug, tel: 725-2202.
Walgreen's, tel: 722-6290.
Farmacías El Amal, 617 Europa, Santurce, tel: 728-1760.
Farmacías Moscoso, Arzuaga Fte Plaza St, Río Piedras, tel: 753-1394.
Walgreens, 1130 Ashford Ave, Condado, tel: 725-1510.
MAYAGÜEZ: Walgreens, Mayagüez Mall, tel: 832-2072.
PONCE: Seedman's, Centro del Sur Shopping Center, tel: 840-7878.

Special Considerations: Puerto Rico has few of the dangerous bacteria and diseases that plague other semi-tropical areas, but one deserves special mention. Almost all of the island's rivers are infected with the bacteria "*chisto,*" which can cause severe damage to internal organs. Some say that river water is safe to drink and swim in on the upper altitudes of mountains, provided it is running swiftly, but this guide does not recommend it. Drinking water is safe.

USEFUL TELEPHONE NUMBERS

SAN JUAN
Police, tel: 343-2020.
Fire, tel: 343-2330.
Medical Center of Puerto Rico, tel: 754-3535.
Assist (for medical emergencies), tel: 343-2222.
Coast Guard, tel: 729-6770.
Rape Hotline, tel: 765-2285.
Poison Treatment Center, tel: 754-8536.
American Red Cross, tel: 759-7979.

GETTING AROUND

DOMESTIC TRAVEL

BY AIR

Puerto Rico is dotted with airports. While most international and many domestic flights to San Juan use **Muñoz Marín Airport** in Isla Verde, many others use San Juan's second airport, **Isla Grande**, just across an estuary south of Puerta de Tierra. Ponce and Mayagüez have modern, if small, airports which give residents 20-minute access to the capital. Also, part of Ramey Air Force Base near Aguadilla has been converted to a civilian airport which serves domestic flights as well as charters and some international flights from Canada. Dorado, only a 45-minute drive west of San Juan, has an airport which services its resorts. Vieques has a fine airport, and the Vieques Air Link, which leaves Isla Grande and costs only $25 each way, is a pleasurable means of getting to and from that charming island.

Small planes can be chartered at Isla Grande Airport.

BY BUS

Puerto Rico's major cities are linked by *públicos*, small vans which assemble at stands all over San Juan and in pre-established locations in the smaller cities. *Públicos* are cheap and comfortable, probably the best alternative to having one's own car.

San Juan, Ponce and Mayagüez have very efficient local bus services. Buses can be hailed at signs reading *Parada de Guaguas*.

TOUR COMPANIES

Borínquen Tours, tel: 725-4990, 725-2460
Fuentes Bus Line, tel: 780-7070
Gray Line Sightseeing Tours, tel: 727-8080
United Tour Guides, tel: 721-3000 ext 2597

WATER TRANSPORT

As Puerto Rico is fairly rectangular in shape, with few awkward peninsulas and bays, it lacks the extensive water transportation networks of other islands in the Caribbean. There are some exceptions: the ferry from the tourist piers of San Juan to Cataño, a mile across San Juan Bay, is a time-saver and a real bargain. Ferries leave the docks at Fajardo twice daily (9.15am and 4.30pm) for Vieques. Ferries from Fajardo to Culebra leave at 4pm Monday through Saturday with a 9am boat on Sundays, Saturdays and holidays. Boats can be chartered in Mayagüez for the arduous but fascinating 45-mile trip to the Isle of Mona.

PRIVATE TRANSPORT

CAR RENTAL

Puerto Rico has one of the highest per capita rates of car ownership in the Americas, and an automobile is a necessity for anyone who wants to see the island extensively. Puerto Rico therefore has an inordinately high concentration of car rental dealerships. A complete listing can be found by looking in the local yellow pages under *Automóviles Alquiler*. Avis, Budget, Hertz and National rental offices are located in the arrival terminal at Muñoz Marín Airport; others are a short shuttle-bus trip away. Most have unlimited mileage. Smaller companies often have excellent automobiles and are less expensive. Insurance is usually extra; be sure to get it, and check the terms of the coverage before signing anything.

Most rental agencies require that you be at least 25 years old and carry a major credit card. Some will take a large cash deposit in lieu of the card. Foreign drivers may need to produce an international driver's license or license from their home country. US licenses are valid in Puerto Rico.

Avis, tel: (800) 331-1212; Isla Verde (airport), tel: 791-0426; Mayagüez, tel: 833-7070; Ponce, tel: 848-4188.
Budget, tel: (800) 527-0700; Condado, tel: 725-1182; Hato Rey, tel: 751-4330.
Charlie, tel: 728-2418.

Discount, tel: 726-1460.
Hertz, tel: (800) 654-3131; Condado, tel: 725-2027; Isla Verde (airport), tel: 791-0840; Puerta de Tierra, tel: 721-0303; Ponce (airport), tel: 842-7377; Mayagüez (airport), tel: 832-3314.
L&M, tel: 725-8307.
National, tel: (800) 328-4567; San Juan, tel: 791-1805.
Target, tel: 783-6592.
Thrifty, tel: (800) 367-2277; Isla Verde (airport), tel: 791-4241.

MOTORING ADVISORIES

Speed limits are not often posted in Puerto Rico. They are listed in miles, paradoxically – distance signs are in kilometers. The speed limit on the San Juan-Ponce *autopista* is 55 mph (90 kph). Limits elsewhere are far lower, especially in residential areas, where speed-bumps (*lomos*) provide a natural barrier to excess.

Puerto Rico's older coastal highways take efficient routes but can be slow going, due to never-ending traffic lights. Roads in the interior are narrow, tortuous, ill-paved, and always dangerous. Often, they run along dizzying cliffsides. Frequent landslides mean that roads often wash out. Slow down if you see a sign reading *Desprendimiento* ("Landslide"). *Desvio* means "detour" and *Carretera Cerrada* means "Road Closed." You'll see plenty of these signs on a trip through the beautiful country roads of the Cordillera. Neither hitchhiking nor picking up hitchhikers is advised.

WHERE TO STAY

Puerto Rico has a wide range of accommodations unusual for a Caribbean island which draws droves of tourists. As one would expect, big resorts set the tone. Still, guest houses, beach houses, grand hotels, flophouses and camping grounds, as well as a host of less conventional settings round out an encouraging, if expensive lodging situation.

Puerto Rico's big resorts are of two types. The first comprises richly equipped, beautifully landscaped beachfront resorts, best typified by the **Caribe Hilton**, grandaddy of the tropical Hiltons, in Puerta de Tierra; the **Hyatt Regency Cerromar**, a Rockefeller–financed resort just west of San Juan in Dorado; Fajardo's **El Conquistador** and Humacao's famous **Palmas del Mar**. These tend to have casinos and several bars. Except for the Caribe Hilton, all have beautifully groomed golf courses. Each is characterized by big swimming pools, excellent facilities for tennis and exercise and long stretches of lovely beachfront. Another thing these places have in common is that they are extremely expensive.

The second tier of resort hotels are somewhat less lavish, may lack casinos and tend to be about half as expensive as the others. These are typified by the big, white high-rises of San Juan's Condado and Isla Verde areas. They tend to cater less exclusively to holiday-makers and draw a more diverse crowd of guests. Many of these are businessmen, and the Condado hotels in particular have made great efforts over the past several years to draw conventions.

Guest houses are perhaps the most pleasant lodging option. These tend to be smaller and more intimate than the resorts, averaging around a dozen rooms. Many of them are on beaches and offer the guest the opportunity to walk across the patio, not a check-out lobby, for a morning swim. About half of these have bars; almost all of them have pools.

There are a certain number of run-down, sleazy hotels, most of them in major cities, which have gone to seed and tend to be full of bugs and dirt. They don't have bars. They're not air-conditioned. They tend to stay in business by boarding illegal immigrants and state-supported residents. They're extremely cheap, however, and the real budget tourist may be persuaded to brave the bugs.

The one unique lodging option Puerto Rico offers is the *parador*. These state-run country farmhouses, often old coffee or sugar *haciendas*, offer the authentic ambience of Puerto Rican rural life. Beautiful old furniture, elegant dining facilities and the opportunity – at some – to pick one's own food for dessert make these well worth trying for those who prefer to see a Puerto Rico that won't remind one of Nice or Miami Beach. They are about the same price as guest houses.

The pricing system below, is based on a double room in winter high season. $$$ means over $250, $$ is $150–250, $ is under $150.

CÓNDADO

Condado Beach Hotel & Casino, 1061 Ashford, tel: 721-6090. Beautiful mansion on outside, government-owned, poorly kept hotel on the inside. Stay here only at a pinch. $$

Condado Plaza Hotel & Casino, 999 Ashford, tel: 721-1000. Centrally located, ideal for business travelers, this is considered Condado's best full-service hotel. Top-notch restaurants, casino, pool (recently remodeled), discotheque and business center. $$$

Dutch Inn & Tower, 55 Condado, tel: 721-0810. Moderately priced hotel two blocks from the beach; casino and popular restaurant, the Green House. $$

El Canario Inn, 1317 Ashford, tel: 722-3861. Charming small hotel near the water; lots of character. $

Marriott San Juan, Ashford. Scheduled for re-opening in mid-1995, this hotel was formerly the Dupont Plaza Hotel & Cosino, which was closed after the New Year's Eve 1986 fire that killed 97 people.

Radisson Ambassador, 1369 Ashford, tel: 721-7300. Formerly Howard Johnson's, still has a famous ice-cream parlor; nice piano bar adjacent to casino. $$

ISLA VERDE

El San Juan Hotel & Casino, Isla Verde, tel: 719-1000. Many consider this Puerto Rico's finest hotel. Lavish resort also has some of San Juan's best restaurants, including Dar Tiffany and Back Street Hong Kong. $$$

Holiday Inn Crowne Plaza, Route 187, Km. 1.5, tel: 253-2929. Near Boca de Cangrejos and Piñones public beaches. $$

Sands Hotel & Casino, Isla Verde, tel: 719-6100. Beautiful, modern, full-service hotel. Las Vegas-style entertainment at night. $$$

PUERTA DE TIERRA

Caribe Hilton, Calle San Jeronimo, tel: 721-0303. The grandaddy of big resorts, the 650-room Caribe Hilton was inaugurated in 1949 and is still the only hotel in Puerto Rico with its own private beach. VIPs and foreign dignitaries usually stay here. $$$

Radisson Normandie, Avenida Muñoz Rivera, tel: 729-2929. Stark white hotel shaped like a boat; some what antiseptic interior. $$

OLD SAN JUAN

Casa San José, 159 San José, tel: 723-1212. A luxuriously restored 300-year-old mansion with 10 sumptuous rooms. $$

El Escenario Guest House, 152 San Sebastián, tel: 721-5264. Charming seven-room guest house above lively bar, this may be Old San Juan's best lodging bargain. Rates include breakfast on rooftop terrace. Ask for Ben or Bella. $

Galeria San Juan, 204 Norzagaray, tel: 722-1808. Art gallery and eight-room guest house in 16th-century mansion restored by sculptor and local personality Jan D'Esopo. $

Gran Hotel El Convento, 100 Cristo, tel: 723-9020. An ancient convent, this building was converted in the 1960s into a 100-room hotel. Ideal base for exploring Old San Juan. $$

Hotel Central, 202 San José, tel: 722-2751. Right off Plaza de Armas; caters mainly to black Caribbean islanders on shopping or business trips. $

Wyndham Old San Juan Hotel & Casino. This 242-room hotel (to be the Old City's largest upon completion in late 1995) is the cornerstone of the ambitious Paseo Portuario – a $125 million, seven-building development supposed to turn Old San Juan's decaying waterfront into a showcase of urban planning. $$$

MIRAMAR

Hotel Excelsior, 801 Ponce de León, tel: 721-7400. Businessman's hotel, easy access to old San Juan, Condado. $$

Hotel Toro, 605 Miramar, tel: 725-5150. Nice choice for budget travelers. $

DORADO

Hyatt Regency Cerromar Dorado Beach, Route 693, tel: 796-1234. Very upscale resort with world-renowned golf course and $3 million pool. Also site of annual Puerto Rico Manufacturers' Association convention. $$$

FAJARDO

El Conquistador Resort & Country Club, Route 987, Km. 4.1, tel: 863-1000. This newly renovated, 918-room resort has everything a well-heeled tourist could want, including a 10-acre private island accessible by ferry boat. $$$

PONCE

Holiday Inn Ponce, Highway 2, Km. 221.2, tel: 844-1200. Part of the international chain; overlooks the Caribbean. $

Hotel Melia, 2 Cristina, tel: 842-0260. Charming hotel in heart of restored district; the ideal place to stay for discovering downtown Ponce. Friendly staff; room price includes breakfast on rooftop terrace. $

Ponce Hilton, Highway 14, tel: 259-7676 or 259-7777. New government-owned hotel, city's most luxurious, has casino and 18-hole golf course. $$

PARADORES

Many of the *paradores* out on the island are restored 19th-century coffee plantations, and are located in particularly scenic areas. Rates are very reasonable, usually not more than $50–60 a night, and the food is often much better than what you would find at nearby restaurants. From the US mainland, *parador* reservations can be made through a central toll-free number, (800) 443-0266. In San Juan, dial 721-2884; from outside the metro area, call (800) 981-7575 toll-free. At the moment, 18 *paradores* are certified by the Puerto Rico Tourism Company.

Baños de Coamo, Coamo, tel: 825-2239
Boquemar, Boquerón, tel: 851-2158
Casa Grande, Utuado, tel: 894-3939
El Faro, Aguadilla, tel: 822-8000
Guajataca, Quebradillas, tel: 895-3070
Hacienda Gripiñas, Jayuya, tel: 828-1717
Hacienda Juanita, Maricao, tel: 838-2550
J B Hidden Village, Aguada, tel: 886-8686
Joyuda Beach, Boquerón, tel: 851-5650
La Familia, Fajardo, tel: 863-1193
Martorell, Luquillo, tel: 889-2710
Oasis, San Germán, tel: 892-1175
Perichi's, Rincón, tel: 851-3131
Posada Porlamar, La Parguera, tel: 899-4015
Sol, Mayagüez, tel: 834-0303
Villa Antonia, Rincón, tel: 823-2645
Villa Parguera, La Parguera, tel: 899-3975
Vistamar, Quebradillas, tel: 895-2065

FOOD DIGEST

WHAT TO EAT

Aside from having a delectable and historic native cuisine, Puerto Rico benefits from its American and Caribbean connections in having just about all the "ethnic" cuisines you'd find in the largest cities of the United States. Spanish, US, Mexican, Chinese, French, Swiss, Brazilian, Japanese and other food is plentiful, especially in San Juan.

Puerto Rican cuisine differs from that of its Spanish neighbors in the Caribbean almost as much as it differs from that of the mainland US. Relying heavily on beans, rice and whatever Puerto Ricans haul out of the sea, it is a mild, filling, well-balanced style of cookery. See the feature on Puerto Rican Cuisine (page 239) for the details.

WHERE TO EAT

You can get Puerto Rican food in all manner of spots: in the modest urban *fondas*, where a rich *asopao de camarones* will run you under five bucks;

in the rural *colmados* where roast chicken is the order of the day; and in the posh restaurants of Old San Juan and the Condado, such as **La Mallorquina**, the Caribbean's oldest continuously operating restaurant. The restaurants of San Juan tend to be concentrated in certain areas.

While *fondas* are all over town, European cuisine tends to be concentrated in the trendier parts of Old San Juan and in the more expensive areas of the Condado and Santurce, such as Ashford Avenue. There must be a higher concentration of American fast-food joints than anywhere else on earth. These are in the Condado and the modern shopping malls in Carolina and Hato Rey. Bars are everywhere.

Pricing system: $$$ – expensive, $$ – moderate, $ – inexpensive.

SAN JUAN

OLD SAN JUAN

Amadeus, 106 San Sebastián, Old San Juan, tel: 722-8635. Puerto Rican. Traditional Puerto Rican dinners, fresh seafood and delicious *ceviche* on Plaza San José. $$

Amanda's, 424 Norzagaray, Old San Juan, tel: 722-1682. Mexican. Nice drinks and ocean view, but French-Mexican dishes and vegetable plates are overpriced. Slow service. $$

Bistro Gambaro, 320 Fortaleza, Old San Juan, tel: 724-4592. Caribbean. Upscale restaurant owned by Patricia Wilson, food columnist for the *San Juan Star*, serves creative entrées such as linguini with pesto and chicken in tamarind sauce. Prices include fresh garden salad and delicious dessert. $$$

Café Berlin, 407 San Francisco, Old San Juan, tel: 722-5205. Vegetarian. Owned by a German baker, this "gourmet vegetarian" eatery fronting Plaza Colón offers fresh pastas, organic foods and delicious salad bar. Portions on the small side. $$

Café Callaloo, 252 Cristo, Old San Juan, tel: 722-3457. Caribbean. Trinidadian-owned sidewalk café offers spicy chicken, pasta salad, goat curry and other Creole specialties; one of the Old City's true dining bargains. $

El Jalapeño, 255 Tetuán, Old San Juan, tel: 723-1679. Mexican. Best Mexican restaurant in the Old City offers friendly service and a wide variety of entrées from Filete Zona Rosa to *fajitas tropicales*, and margaritas that will knock your *sombreros* off. $$

Hard Rock Café, 253 Recinto Sur, Old San Juan, tel: 724-7625. American. Crammed like all other Hard Rocks with musical memorabilia, this restaurant also features delicious food (try the "veggie burger"), large video screens and surprisingly quick service. Great Old San Juan dining experience – if you can stand the noise. $

La Bombonera, 259 San Francisco, Old San Juan, tel: 722-0658. Puerto Rican. Traditional cafeteria-style bakery and the best place in Old San Juan for a cheap, satisfying *arroz con pollo* and coffee with local pastry. $

La Chaumière, 367 Tetuán, Old San Juan, tel: 722-3330. French. The Old City's only French restaurant offers treats such as baby rack of lamb with herbs, scallopine of veal with medallion of lobster topped with asparagus and Béarnaise sauce. Very expensive; reservations requested. $$$

La Mallorquina, 207 San Justo, Old San Juan, tel: 722-3261. Puerto Rican. Oldest restaurant in Puerto Rico, dating from 1848. House specialties are *asopao de marisco* and *arroz con pollo*. Worth a visit if only for interior courtyard. Reservations recommended. $$

La Zaragozana, 356 San Francisco, Old San Juan, tel: 723-5103. Spanish. Fancy Spanish restaurant featuring dishes like filet of pork and *pollo andaluza*. Big bucks, slow service. $$$

Maria's, 202 Cristo, Old San Juan. Mexican. Nice bar, but Mexican-style food tastes like plastic and "tropical drinks" are mostly artificial. Popular with cruise ship employees. $

Yukiyu, 311 Recinto Sur, Old San Juan, tel: 721-0653. Oriental. Japanese *Teppanyaki* restaurant and *shushi* lover's paradise. Expensive; reservations required. $$$

PUERTA DE TIERRA

El Hamburger, 402 Muñoz Rivera, Puerta de Tierra, tel: 725-5891. American. Rustic eatery overlooking the Atlantic; nearly blown away by Hurricane Hugo in 1989. Enjoy the best flame-broiled burgers in town while listening to guitar-playing "Calypso Man." $

Marisqueria Atlantica, 7 Lugo Vinas, Puerta de Tierra, tel: 722-0890. Seafood. Prides itself on "friendliest fresh food and fish restaurant in town".

CONDADO & OCEAN PARK

C'est La Vie, Ashford and Magdalena, Condado, tel: 721-6075. French. Indoor-outdoor café on Condado's Plaza de la Libertad. Features crépes, *fajitas*, sirloin burgers; pricey. $$

Cadillac Café, 1021 Ashford, Condado, tel: 725-4930. American. One of the few places in Puerto

Rico offering hot pastrami sandwiches, meatball subs and other New York-style deli food. Nice clean atmosphere. $

Chart House, 1214 Ashford, Candado, tel: 728-0110. Steak and seafood. Fresh seafood, prime-rib restaurant with verandahs looking out over tropical garden. Popular yuppie hangout. $$$

Compostela, 106 Ave. Condado, tel: 724-6088. Spanish. Rated "excellent" by *San Juan City Magazine*, which recommends royal pheasant with raspberry sauce and chocolate-and-coffee mousse for dessert. $$$

Dunbar's, 1954 McLeary, Ocean Park, tel: 728-2920. American. Favorite *gringo* hangout and pick-up joint with buffalo chicken wings and dart games.

L K Sweeney and Son, Condado Plaza Hotel, tel: 723-5551. Seafood. Baked stuffed Maine lobster, seafood stew are house specialties at Sweeney's, which also boasts the Caribbean's largest oyster bar. Nice piano bar; reservations recommended. $$$

Lotus Flower, Condado Plaza Hotel, tel: 722-0940. Oriental. The *New York Times* hails this as one of the very best restaurants in Puerto Rico. Features Szechuan, Hunan, Mandarin and Cantonese cuisine, and the only *dim sum* on the island. Reservations recommended. $$$

Via Appia, 1350 Ashford, Condado, tel: 725-8711. Italian. Sidewalk café featuring pizza and basic pasta dishes. $

HATO REY & RÍO PIEDRAS

Jerusalem Restaurant, O'Neill I-6, Hato Rey, tel: 764-3265. Arabic. Palestinian owners offer Arabic delights such as grilled leg of lamb, stuffed grape leaves and cardamom coffee; Arab grocery and video store in back. $$

Middle East Restaurant, 207 Padre Colón, Río Piedras, tel: 751-7304. Arabic. Nicely decorated eatery in heart of San Juan's tiny "Arab Quarter," specializes in *felafel*, *hummus* and full course traditional Arabic dinners; belly-dancing on weekend nights. $$

SANTURCE

Casita Blanca, 351 Tapia, Santurce, tel: 726-5501. Puerto Rican. Outstanding local cuisine in café restaurant with outdoor patio, located, unfortunately, in one of Santurce's worst neighborhoods. Its specialties, from *gandinga* to *pastelón de amarillo*, have been mentioned in both *Gourmet* magazine and *The New York Times*. $

La Casona, 609 San Jorge, esq. Fernández Juncos, Santurce, tel: 727-2717. Spanish. Very expensive restaurant in an old Spanish-style home replete with tropical gardens and immaculate service. Lobster salad, stuffed rabbit loin and the best *paella* in Puerto Rico make this a popular lunch or dinner spot – especially for executives on expense accounts. $$$

ISLA VERDE

Back Street Hong Kong, El San Juan Hotel, tel: 791-1224. Oriental. Set in a pagoda used as the Hong Kong Pavilion in the 1962 New York World's Fair. Besides delicious Mandarin, Szechuan and Hunan dishes, this restaurant features huge salt-water aquarium and 19th-century Chinese antiques. Excellent service, reasonable prices; reservations required. $$$

Dar Tiffany, El San Juan Hotel, Isla Verde, tel: 791-7272. Steak and seafood. Winner of prestigious awards by Puerto Rico's two biggest newspapers, this is one of San Juan's best restaurants. Dry-aged prime beef, Maine lobster, fresh seafood and extensive wine list make this a favorite. $$$

Lupi's, Route 187, Km. 1.3, Isla Verde, tel: 253-2198. Mexican. Mexican bar and sports *cantina* with a decidedly American flavor. Delicious *fajitas* and flying fish, and best margaritas in San Juan; impeccable service. $

CATAÑO

La Casita, 27 Manuel Enrique, Cataño, tel: 788-5080. Seafood. Fancy restaurant in a very poor neighborhood serves delicious fresh fish; specialties include octopus cocktail and *mofongo relleno* with lobster. $$$

CULTURE PLUS

MUSEUMS

Casa del Callejón, Callejon de la Capilla and Fortaleza St, Old San Juan, tel: 721-1689.

Casa del Libro, 255 Cristo St, Old San Juan, tel: 723-0354. A beautiful collection of old manuscripts and documents dating from the days of San Juan's founding, as well as some of Puerto Rico's best modern graphic work, in a charming old house. Open: 11am – 4.30pm Monday to Friday. Admission: free.

Museum of Fine Arts, 253 Cristo St, Old San Juan, tel: 724-5998. A huge disappointment, with only second-rate modern exhibits usually on display in one small room. Open: 9am–noon and 1pm–4pm daily except Monday and Thursday. Admission: free.

Museum of the Americas, Old San Juan. Located in the restored Ballajá barracks, this museum offers an overview of cultural, development in the New World. It features changing exhibitions, archaeological finds of the Ballajá area and Latin American/ Caribbean crafts exhibits. Open 10am–4pm Tuesday to Friday, 11am–5pm weekends. Admission: free.

Museum of the Seas, Pier One, Old San Juan, tel: 725-2532. Lots of maritime tools and exhibits, as well as maps, from the Age of Sail. Open: when cruise ships dock. Admission: free.

Pablo Casals Museum, 101 San Sebastián St, Old San Juan, tel: 723-9185. A tiny, innovative museum crammed with memorabilia of the great cellist who made Puerto Rico his home. Highlights include manuscripts and mementos of Casals's involvement with the United Nations. Videotapes of Casals concerts played on request. Open: 9am–5pm Tuesday to Saturday, 1pm–4pm Sunday. Admission: free.

Pharmacy Museum, Casa de los Contrafuertes, Old San Juan, tel: 724-5998. A 19th-century pharmacy reassembled in the oldest house in the city. Open: 9am–noon, 1pm–4.30pm except Monday. Admission: free.

Ponce Art Museum, Las Americas Ave, Ponce, tel: 848-0505. An art museum of staggering scope and beauty, with major works of many of the great figures of European art. Excellent works from Rubens, Van Dyck, Gainsborough and others in a visionary building of hexagonal rooms designed by Edward Durrell Stone. Open: 10am–noon and 1pm–4pm Monday to Friday, 10am–4pm Saturday, 10am–5pm Sunday. Admission: $3 adults, $2 children.

San Juan Museum of Art and History, Norzagaray St, Old San Juan, tel: 724-1875. In two rooms and tinier than this city deserves, but a good primer on the relationship between the creative arts and the development of the city. Open: 8am–noon, 1pm–4pm Monday to Friday. Admission: free.

Tibes Indian Ceremonial Center, Route 503, Km. 2.7, Tibes, tel: 840-2255. A 1,500-year-old Taíno village excavated in 1975, remarkably intact, with plazas, *bateyes*, and a rock ring possibly used as an astronomical observatory. Informative guides and

museum. Open: 9am–4.30pm except Monday. Admission: $2 adults, 50¢ children.

ART GALLERIES

Almost all of Puerto Rico's cities sell their native crafts, from Aguadillan lace to Loízan *veigante* masks, but an art "scene," as understood in New York, exists only in San Juan. Here, the combination of a radiant light and an active network of patronage have worked to draw most of the finest painters of Puerto Rico and many from North America and Europe. Sculpture thrives, as do the crafts of Puerto Rico and other Latin-American nations. Most galleries are huddled together on a few of Old San Juan's streets, but you'll find plenty of pleasant surprises in San Juan's other neighborhoods and even out on the island. Here are some of the better spots in the metropolitan area:

Art Students' League, San José St, Old San Juan, tel: 722-4468. A small, changing display of some of San Juan's up-and-coming artists, with a tendency towards the vanguard and the experimental. Open: 8am–4pm Monday to Saturday.

Galería Diego, 51 Maria Moczo St, Ocean Park, tel: 728-1287. Changing exhibits of local painting and sculpture. Open: 10am–6pm Monday to Friday, until 9pm on Thursday, and 10am–1pm Saturday.

Galería Labiosa, 312 San Francisco St, Old San Juan, tel: 721-2848. Paintings and sculpture. Open: 9.30am–5pm Monday to Saturday.

Galería Palomas, 207 Cristo St, Old San Juan, tel: 724-8904. A fine collection of Puerto Rican paintings and graphic design. Open: 10am–6pm Monday to Saturday.

Galería San Juan, 204-206 Norzagaray St, Old San Juan, tel: 722-1808. A sizable changing collection of fine paintings in an elegant, old building. Work has a tendency away from the abstract. Open: 10am–5pm Tuesday to Saturday.

Galerías Botello, 208 Cristo St, Old San Juan, tel: 723-9987. Fine Haitian paintings, among other things, in an artist-operated gallery. Open: 10am–6pm Monday to Saturday.

CONCERTS

The San Juan Symphony Orchestra has progressed in a few short years to a position of great respectability. Frequent concerts are held in the Fine Arts Center Festival Hall, known locally as the "Bellas Artes," in Santurce. Chamber music ensembles are numerous at the university and among private concert-givers. The highlight of the classical music year comes in early June, when the San Juan Symphony's performances at Bellas Artes are complemented by guest appearances from musicians from around the world, some of them as renowned as Yitzhak Perlman and Maxim Shostakovich.

BALLETS

There are plenty of opportunities to see ballet in San Juan. The Friends of San Juan Ballet periodically host performances with the Symphony Orchestra at Bellas Artes. The San Juan City Ballet are frequent performers at the restored Tapia y Rivera Theater in Old San Juan, and give matinee performances. Rounding out dance offerings are the modern dance shows given at the Julia de Burgos Amphitheater in Río Piedras as part of the UPR Cultural Activities.

LIBRARY

Puerto Rico is not long on public libraries; most are in universities and private foundations, and much exchange of books rests on person-to-person lending. Here are a few exceptions:

Ateneo Puertorriqueño, Ponce de León, Stop 2, Puerta de Tierra, tel: 722-4839.
Volunteer Library League, 250 Ponce de León, Santurce, tel: 725-7672.

MOVIES

Puerto Rico is woefully understocked with movie theaters, even in San Juan. A handful in Santurce show first-runs and oldies, but it's best to look them up in the phone directory under "*Cinemas*" to find out what's playing on the day.

Good films can be seen at unexpected places, however. The Amphitheaters at the University of Puerto Rico frequently show art films, especially in the UPR Cultural Activities series, whose showings are at 5pm and 8pm every Tuesday. For more information, tel: 764-0000, ext 2563.

NIGHTLIFE

The nightlife of Puerto Rico ranges from the tranquility of coffee and conversation to the steamy, fast-lane excesses of San Juan's clubs. On cool nights in the Cordillera, nightlife resembles what one assumes Puerto Ricans have enjoyed for decades, if not centuries. Townspeople gather round local plazas and sing to the accompaniment of guitars, finding time between tunes for a couple of sips of Bacardí or Medalla.

San Juan duplicates much of this rural nightlife – on weekends in the old city, youths of high school and college age mill about the Plaza San José by the hundreds, stopping in bars and restaurants and coffee houses, and trying to get groups together to go dancing.

But in San Juan and other cities, partying is in general taken with more reckless abandon. The whole city is crowded with bars and dancing establishments of all description. In Old San Juan, **El Batey**, **Los Hijos de Borínquen** and **El Patio de Sam** provide good spots for drinking and talk. In Santurce, **Shannan's** is crowded with hard-drinking, hard-rocking *norteamericanos*. Those who wish to opt out of such hedonism would do well to sip a cup of coffee in one of Old San Juan's finer establishments like Café Violeta, a quiet piano bar on Fortaleza Street.

NIGHTSPOTS

Amadeus, 106 San Sebastián, Old San Juan.
El Batey, Cristo St, Old San Juan. Best bar on the island. Small, loud, great juke-box. Open until 6am.
Hard Rock Café, 253 Recinto Sur, Old San Juan, tel: 724-7625. Delicious food and loud music, with lots of rock-n-roll memorabilia.
Isadora's Discotheque, Holiday Inn, 999 Ashford Ave, Condado, tel: 721-1000. Busy, late night, singles' hangout.
Krash, 1257 Ponce de León, Santurce, tel: 722-1390. Caters to homosexuals.
Laser's, 251 Calle Cruz, tel: 721-4479. Loud teen disco.
Lupi's, Route 187, Km. 1.3, Isla Verde, tel: 253-2198. Mexican bar and sports *cantina*. Delicious margaritas, fabulous *fajitas* and live music.
Maria's, 204 Cristo St, Old San Juan. Singles' bar.
Shannan's Irish Pub, 1503 Loíza, Santurce, tel: 728-6103. San Juan's Irish bar, with two pool tables and nightly hard rock live. Air-conditioning.
Small World, San José St, Old San Juan. Expats' drinking hangout.
1919 Lounge, Condado Beach Hotel, Condado, tel: 725-2302. Ritzy piano bar. Open until 3am.

GAMBLING

Gambling is legal in Puerto Rico. Casinos offer blackjack, roulette, poker, slot machines and all manner of games of chance, though they have somewhat lost their novelty for US visitors since the laws were liberalized in the States.

Casinos are permitted only in hotels, and tend to be open from mid-evening until early morning. Jackets and ties are often mandatory. The following hotels in San Juan, Dorado and Humacao have casinos:

Ambassador, Condado
Caribe Hilton, Puerta de Tierra
Caribe Inn, Isla Verde
Condado Beach, Condado
Condado Plaza, Condado
Dutch Inn, Condado
El Conquistador, Fajardo
El San Juan, Isla Verde
Mayagüez Hilton, Mayagüez
Palace, Isla Verde
Ponce Hilton, Ponce
Quality Royale, Miramar
Ramada, Condado
Sands, Isla Verde

DORADO

Hyatt Dorado Beach
Hyatt Regency Cerromar

HUMACAO

Palmas del Mar

SHOPPING

In San Juan, the more upmarket shopping areas tend to be concentrated in the Old City and the Condado. Old San Juan boasts the more boutiquey atmosphere of the two. It is probably also what one could call more "authentic," with plenty of shops selling tourist baubles, curios, T-shirts and various other items. Among the better stores in the Old City are its jewelry shops, especially numerous along Fortaleza Street, which have signs reading "Joyería." Other specialties include leather and various arts and crafts, ancient and modern. **Gonzalez Padín**, the oldest department store on the island, is located right in the middle of town.

The Condado lures customers with slightly more money to spend, and thus sells more goods of lasting value. Clothing, porcelain, crystal, jewelry – each is represented in at least a handful of shops which are called "Boutique" or "Shoppe." There's less of a marketplace ambience in Condado, and a decidedly touristic tone to the merchandise there.

Hato Rey, Santurce and Isla Verde are more workaday marketplaces for permanent residents, places you'd go to buy a refrigerator or a television or a car.

An exception is **Plaza de Las Américas**, the Caribbean's largest shopping mall, in Hato Rey. This is the best place on the island to go for *norteamericano* merchandise. It is rivalled by the **Plaza Carolina** shopping center in Carolina. Other malls exist on the island, like the **Centro del Sur** in Ponce and the **Mayagüez Mall** in Mayagüez. Cities as small as Caguas and Cayey have malls of good size.

For traditional (barter) shopping in San Juan, the best marketplace is the **Plaza del Mercado**, a bustling outdoor affair in Río Piedras. Primarily a fruit market, the Plaza del Mercado nonetheless trucks in merchandise of all kinds. Prices are often unlisted and haggling can be intense. Miramar has a smaller market on the same model.

BOOKSTORES

The following have a good selection of books in both English and Spanish:

B. Dalton, Plaza Carolina, Carolina, tel: 752-1275.
Bell, 102 De Diego Ave, Santurce, tel: 728-5000.
Bookword, Plaza Las Américas, Hato Rey, tel: 753-7140.
Casa Papyrus, 357 Tetuán, Old San Juan, tel: 724-6555.
Cultural Puertorriqueña, 1406 Fernández Juncos, Stop 20, Santurce, tel: 721-5683.
Librería Hispanoamericana, 1013 Ponce de León, Río Piedras, tel: 763-3415.
Librería La Tertulia, Amalia Marín and González, Río Piedras, tel: 765-1148.
The Book Store, 255 San José, Old San Juan, tel: 724-1815.
Thekes, Plaza de las Américas, Hato Rey, tel: 765-1539.

SPORTS

PARTICIPANT

SWIMMING

Puerto Rico is ringed with sandy beaches, some of them outrageously popular, others secluded and quiet. Many are *balnearios*, public bathing facilities complete with life-guards, refreshment stands, dressing rooms and parking lots. Of those around San Juan, the most popular are probably those at **Luquillo** and **Vega Baja**. But all of Puerto Rico's beaches are exceptional, and all beachfront – with the exception of the Caribe Hilton – is public. Swimmers are advised to be careful of strong surf and undertow at certain beaches, especially in the northwest.

SURFING

Puerto Rico has almost ideal conditions for surfing – warm water, brilliant sunshine and heavy but even tubular surf. Many of the most popular spots are convenient to San Juan: **Piñones**, off Route 187 in Isla Verde, is probably the most renowned, and **Aviones**, so named because of the airplanes that fly over from nearby Muñoz Marín Airport, is just a bit farther down the road in Piñones. In the northwest, **Punta Higüero**, off Route 413 in Rincón, is world famous, and hosted surfing's world championships a few years ago. In the southwest, Jobos Beach proves popular among Mayagüez residents.

SCUBA & SNORKELING

Ringed by a submarine forest of coral and subject to some of the greatest variations in underwater depth in the world, Puerto Rico is prime scuba territory for those with the expertise. Those who would like to learn scuba in San Juan can get lessons at:

Caribbean School of Aquatics, 1 Taft St, Suite 10-F Condado, tel: 723-4740.
Caribe Aquatic Adventure, Caribe Hilton, Puerta de Tierra, tel: 724-1307.

OUT ON THE ISLAND

FAJARDO: Carlos A. Flores, Puerto Chico Marina, tel: 863-0834.
ISABELA: La Cueva Submarina, Plaza Cooperative, tel: 872-3903.

Fajardo is probably the island's capital for water sports. For a relaxing sailing and diving adventure and an exploration of some of the smaller cays off Puerto Rico's east coast, contact: **Jack Becker**, Villa Marina Yacht Harbor, Fajardo, tel: 863-1905.

Snorkeling is also popular among diving pikers. Equipment can be rented or purchased at most dive shops and in certain department stores.

SAILING & WINDSURFING

Most of Puerto Rico's sailors head to Fajardo for weekends on the water. Boats of all sizes and descriptions are available for rental. For more information, consult:

Villa Marina, tel: 863-5131.
Puerto Chico, tel: 863-0834.

Windsurfing is popular all over the island. Boards can be rented at most dive shops, including some of those listed above.

FRESHWATER FISHING

Freshwater fishing has existed in Puerto Rico's 12 man-made lakes for years, but the sport itself has only become popular in the last decade or so.

Some 14 clubs fish the dozen lakes, which were constructed in the 1930s as a source of drinking water and irrigation. Bass, both large-mouth and peacock, are local favorites, though at least seven other native species are fished as well. Plastic worms are the most popular choice of bait among bass fishermen. The lakes are stocked with more than 2,000 baby fish from the Maricao Fish Hatchery (*Los Viveros* in Spanish), an interesting site in itself.

Here's a list of the island's 12 freshwater lakes and the clubs that fish them.

Carraizo (Loíza) Lake: At 84 sq. kilometers the island's largest lake, Carraizo is bordered by Caguas, Gurabo and Trujillo Alto and is accessible by Routes 175 and 739. (Gurabo Fishing Club)
La Plata Lake: Measuring 67 sq. kilometers, this is Puerto Rico's second-largest lake. It is located between Toa Alta, Bayamón and Naranjito, and accessible by Route 167. (San Juan Bass and Bayamón Fishing Club)
Cidra Lake: only 3 sq. kilometers, this is one of the island's smallest lakes. It's between Bayamón and Cidra along Route 172. (Cidra Fishing Club)
Carite Lake: Off Route 179, Carite Lake is located near Guayama and the Carite National Forest. (Guyama Fishing Club)
Toa Vaca Lake: Just south of Villalba off Route 150, but to fish in here, you need a permit from the Water and Sewer Authority. (Freshwater Fishing Federation)
Guayabal Lake: Measuring 16 sq. kilometers and located in the Barrio Pastillo section of Juana Díaz. (Southern Bass Fishermen)
Caonillas Lake: South of Utuado, this lake covers 19 sq. kilometers and can be reached by Route 607. (Utuado Fishing Club)
Dos Bocas Lake: At 41 sq. kilometers, this unusually shaped lake is the third largest in Puerto Rico. It is located between Arecibo and Utuado just off Route 10. (Fishing Association)
Garzas Lake: Located off Route 518 in Adjuntas and among the island's smallest lakes. (Adjuntas Fishing Club)
Guayo Lake: Located in Lares, right off Route 129. (no local club)
Guajataca Lake: Off Route 119 in San Sebastián. (Backlash Fishing Club and Lares Bass Fishing Club)
Yauco Lake: Fed by the Yauco River and located four miles outside the town of Yauco. (no local club)

GOLF & TENNIS

Golf courses and tennis courts are scattered throughout the island, though most of the better ones are in the larger, more expensive resorts. There are certain arrangements, however, which one can make with these resorts to use their courts and courses on a user-fee basis.

Among the resorts with 18-hole championship golf courses are:

Hyatt Regency Cerromar Beach, Dorado, tel: 796-1234, ext. 3013.
Hyatt Dorado Beach, Dorado, tel: 796-1234, ext. 3239.
Palmas del Mar, Humacao, tel: 852-6000, ext. 2525.

SPECTATOR

Puerto Rico has a national pastime – it is baseball. The island has produced some of the greatest stars ever to play the game, and you can find someone to talk baseball with in almost any bar. The **Caribbean League** season runs from October to March, and there are teams in the largest cities. Many aspiring big-leaguers (and not a few has-beens) play in Puerto Rico. Games are almost daily, and tickets generally inexpensive. Those who want to keep abreast of American and National League action will find complete box scores in all the local papers. Also, Atlanta Braves games are televised on certain national stations.

Basketball is another team sport popular on the island; the *Federación Nacional de Baloncesta de Puerto Rico* has teams in almost all the island's larger cities.

Horse racing in San Juan is at **El Comandante Racetrack** in Canóvanas, 10 miles (15 km) east of the city. Races are held on Wednesdays, Fridays and Sundays at 2.30pm; small admission charge. For more information on races, tel: 724-6060.

For a truly Puerto Rican sporting experience, cockfighting is hard to match. Although the sport seems inhumane to many, its popularity on the island cannot be denied. In this sport, dozens of the proudest local cocks are matched one-on-one in a tiny ring, or *gallera*. The predominantly male crowds at most events are almost as interesting as the fights themselves. These highly knowledgeable enthusiasts are often familiar with a cock's pedigree through several generations. The shouts are deafening, the drinking is reckless, and the betting is heavy. Betting is done on a gentlemanly system of verbal agreement, and hundreds of dollars can change hands on a single fight.

Gallerias are scattered all over, and the fights in even the most rural areas can draw hundreds. Admission can be expensive but the beer is cheap. For information on cockfighting in the San Juan area, consult:

Club Gallistico de Puerto Rico, Carr. Isla Verde, Isla Verde, tel: 791-1557.
Club Gallistico Río Piedras, Km 4.2. Carr. 844, Trujillo Alto, tel: 760-8815.

LANGUAGE

The language of Puerto Rico is Spanish. While it is by no means true that "everyone there speaks English," a majority of Puerto Ricans certainly do, especially in San Juan. Almost everyone in a public service occupation will be able to help in either language.

The Puerto Rican dialect of Spanish resembles that of other Antillean islands, and differs from the Iberian dialect in its rapidity, phoneme quality and elisions. For a more detailed look at this rich tongue, see our feature *Let's Hablar Boricua* (page 230).

There are many excellent Spanish-English dictionaries, but **Barron's**, edited at the University of Chicago, is particularly recommended for its sensitivity to the vocabulary and syntax of the Latin-American idiom. Cristine Gallo's *The Language of the Puerto Rican Street* is an exhaustive lexicon of the kind of Puerto Rican slang most dictionaries would blanch at printing.

USEFUL ADDRESSES

TOURIST INFORMATION

Puerto Rico's tourism information facilities are unpredictable but generally worth a visit. The Puerto Rico Tourism Company has its main office at La Princesa, Old San Juan (tel: 721-2400). The best source of printed information on Puerto Rico tourism is **Qué Pasa**, the free booklet published each month by the Tourism Company. For a copy, write: Qué Pasa, Box 4435, Old San Juan Station, San Juan, PR 00905.

Because Puerto Rico isn't an independent nation, it can't have diplomatic relations with anyone. Hence, there are no embassies in San Juan – but plenty of consulates and honorary consulates.

Argentina: Edif Royal Bank Center #828, Hato Rey, tel: 754-6500.
Austria: Edif Olympic Tower #5A, Condado, tel: 791-2521.
Belgium: 1250 Ponce de León 1250, Suite #713, Santurce, tel: 725-3179.
Belize: Ramón Gandía 567, Hato Rey, tel: 250-6600.
Bolivia: Kings Court #52, Condado, tel: 727-6637.
Brazil: Muñoz Rivera 268, Hato Rey, tel: 754-7983.
Canada: Scotiabank Plaza, Piso 13, Hato Rey, tel: 250-0367.
Chile: Edif American Airlines #800, Santurce, tel: 725-6365.
Colombia: Edif Mercantil Plaza #818, Hato Rey, tel: 754-6885.
Costa Rico: Pasionaria 1890, Río Piedras, tel: 759-9048.
Denmark: San Francisco 360, Old San Juan, tel: 725-2514.
Dominican Republic: Edif Avianca, Piso 7, Santurce, tel: 725-9554.
Ecuador: Roosevelt 651, Suite #3A, Miramar, tel: 781-4408.
El Salvador: Calle 4-B-1 Altos, Parkside, Caparra, tel: 793-7576.
Finland: Urb. Torremolinos DG-6, Guaynabo, tel: 257-1144.
France: Edif Mercantil Plaza #720, Hato Rey, tel: 753-1700.
Germany: Santa Bibliana 1618, Río Piedras, tel: 755-8228.
Guatemala: Edif Marina #304-B, Gauynabo, tel: 782-0558.
Iceland: Calle Islandia 2, Bayamón, tel: 786-7171.
Italy: Amatista 93, Río Piedras, tel: 793-5284.
Japan: Edif Banco Popular, Piso 5, Old San Juan, tel: 721-4667.
Mexico: Edif Bankers Finance #1837, Hato Rey, tel: 764-0258.
Netherlands: Bori 1534, Río Piedras, tel: 759-9400.
Nicaragua: Ponce de León 1205, Santurce, tel: 725-7505.
Norway: San Francisco 360, Old San Juan, tel: 725-2514.
Paraguay: Ashford 1350, Apt R1-A, Condado, tel: 724-3056.
Peru: Ponce de León 268, #1009, Hato Rey, tel: 250-0391.
Philippines: Carr 65 Infantaría, Km. 9.7, Carolina, tel: 762-2855
Portugal: Edif ITT Intermedia, Río Piedras, tel: 766-4351.
Spain: Edif Mercantil Plaza, Hato Rey, tel: 758-6090.

Sweden: Apartado 2748, San Juan, tel: 721-4355.
Switzerland: Loíza 1505, Santurce, tel: 727-2978.
Thailand: Costa Rica 159, Hato Rey, tel: 751-0151.
Uruguay: Himalaya 254, Río Piedras, tel: 764-7941.
Venezuela: Edif Mercantil Plaza #601, Hato Rey, tel: 766-4250.

FURTHER READING

GEOGRAPHY & NATURAL HISTORY

Worlds Collide on Vieques: An Intimate Portrait from Time of Columbus, by Elizabeth Langhorne. New York: Rivercross (1992)
Insight Pocket Guide: Puerto Rico, by Larry and Ani Luxner. Hong Kong: Apa Publications (1994)
Ponce: Rebirth of a Valuable Heritage, by Loretta Phelps de Cordova. San Juan: Publishing Resources (1991)
A Guide to the Birds of Puerto Rico and the Virgin Islands, by Herbert Rafaela. Princeton: Princeton University Press (1989)
The Other Puerto Rico, by Kathryn Robinson. San Juan: Permanent Press (1992)

HISTORY & POLITICS

Breakthrough from Colonialism: An Interdisciplinary Study of Statehood. Río Piedras: Editorial de la Universidad de Puerto Rico (1984)
Puerto Rico: A Colonial Experiment, by Raymond Carr. New York: Random (1984)
Puerto Rico: A Political and Cultural History, by Arturo Morales Carrión (editor). New York: W.W. Norton (1983)
Colonial Dilemma: Critical Perspectives on Contemporary Puerto Rico, by Meléndez, Edwin and Elgardo (editors). Boston: South End Press (1993)
The Disenchanted Island: Puerto Rico and the United States in the 20th Century, by Ronald Fernández. New York: Praeger (1992)
Puerto Rico: An Unfinished Story, by Denis J. Hauptly. New York: Antheneum (1991)
Puerto Rico's Statehood Movement, by Edgardo Meléndez. Westport: Greenwood Press (1988)
Five Centuries in Puerto Rico: Portraits and Eras, by Loretta Phelps de Cordova. San Juan Publishing Resources (1993)
The Taínos: Rise and Decline of the People Who Greeted Columbus, by Irving Rouse. New Haven:

Yale University Press (1992)

Requiem on Cerro Maravilla, by Manny Suárez, and Tomás Stella. Maplewood: Waterfront Press (1987)

The Supreme Court and Puerto Rico: The Doctrine of Separate and Unequal, by Juan R. Torruella. Río Piedras: Editorial de la Universidad de Puerto Rico (1986)

The Puerto Ricans: A Documentary History, by Kal Wagenheim and Olga Jiménez de Wagenheim (editors). Princeton: Markus Wiener Publishing (1993)

Puerto Rico's Revolt for Independence: El Grito de Lares, by Olga Jiménez de Wagenheim. Princeton: Markus Wiener Publishing (1993)

ECONOMICS

Tradition Into the Future: The First Century of the Banco Popular de Puerto Rico 1893–1993, by Guillermo A. Baralt. San Juan: Carimar (1993)

Puerto Rico: Development by Integration to the United States, by Eliezer Curet. Río Piedras: Editorial Cultural (1986)

Economic History of Puerto Rico: Institutional Change and Capitalist Development, by James L. Dietz. Princeton: Princeton University Press (1986)

Capitalism in Colonial Puerto Rico, by Teresita Martinéz-Vergne. Gainesville: University of Florida Press (1992)

Labor in the Puerto Rican Economy, by Carlos E. Santiago. New York. Praeger (1992)

CUISINE

Puerto Rican Dishes, by Berta Cabanillas and Carmen Ginorio. Río Piedras: Editorial de la Universidad de Puerto Rico (1993)

The Spirit of Puerto Rican Rum: Recipes and Recollections, by Blanche Gelabert. San Juan: Discovery Press (1992)

Puerto Rican Cuisine in America, by Oswald Rivera. New York: Four Walls Eight Windows (1993)

Rice and Beans and Tasty Things: A Puerto Rican Cookbook, by Dora Pomano. San Juan (1986)

Puerto Rican Cookery, by Carmen Aboy Valldejuli. Gretna: Pelican Publishing (1993)

ARTS, CUSTOMS & SOCIAL LIFE

Puerto Rican Woman, by Edna Acosta-Belén and Eli H. Christensen. New York: Praeger (1979)

Divided Borders: Essays on Puerto Rican Identity, by Juan Flores. Houston: Arte Publico (1993)

Puerto Rican Culture: An Introduction, by Raoul Gordon. New York: Gordon Books (1982)

Antonin Nechodoma, Architect 1877–1928, by Thomas S. Marvel. Gainesville: University of Florida Press (1994)

Puerto Rico 1900: Turn-of-the-Century Architecture in the Hispanic Caribbean, by Jorge Rigau. New

York: Rizzoli (1992)

Trapped: Puerto Rico Families and Schizophrenia, by Lloyed H. Rogler and August B. Hollingshead. Maplewood: Waterfront Press (1985)

When I Was Puerto Rican, by Esmeralda Santiago. Reading: Addison-Wesley Publishing (1993)

FICTION

Family Installments, by Edward Rivera. New York: Morrow (1982)

Macho Camacho's Beat, by Luis Rafael Sánchez. New York: Pantheon (1981)

OTHER INSIGHT GUIDES

Other *Insight Guides* which highlight destinations in this region are:

The vivid text and spectacular photography of *Insight Guide: Caribbean* brings to life the serenity, the allure, and the diversity of the Lesser Antilles islands.

An expert team of writers and photographers, including well-known Bahamians, explains the allure of the 700 islands that make up the beautiful Bahamas.

ART/PHOTO CREDITS

INDEX

A
B
C
D
E
F
G
H
I
J
a
b
c
d
e
f
g
h
i
j
k
l